Health Care Expenditures, Innovation, and Demographic Change

AF756473

Frankfurter Schriften zur Gesundheitspolitik und zum Gesundheitsrecht

Schriftenreihe des Instituts
für Europäische Gesundheitspolitik und Sozialrecht
an der Johann Wolfgang Goethe-Universität Frankfurt

Herausgegeben von Ingwer Ebsen
und Roland Eisen

Band 7

PETER LANG
Frankfurt am Main · Berlin · Bern · Bruxelles · New York · Oxford · Wien

Yasemin Ilgin

Health Care Expenditures, Innovation, and Demographic Change

PETER LANG
Internationaler Verlag der Wissenschaften

Bibliographic Information published by the Deutsche Nationalbibliothek
The Deutsche Nationalbibliothek lists this publication in the Deutsche Nationalbibliografie; detailed bibliographic data is available in the internet at <http://www.d-nb.de>.

Zugl.: Frankfurt (Main), Univ., Diss., 2007

Gedruckt mit freundlicher Unterstützung des
Instituts für Europäische Gesundheitspolitik
und Sozialrecht – ineges.

D 30
ISSN 1610-899X
ISBN 978-3-631-58154-4

© Peter Lang GmbH
Internationaler Verlag der Wissenschaften
Frankfurt am Main 2008
All rights reserved.

All parts of this publication are protected by copyright. Any utilisation outside the strict limits of the copyright law, without the permission of the publisher, is forbidden and liable to prosecution. This applies in particular to reproductions, translations, microfilming, and storage and processing in electronic retrieval systems.

www.peterlang.de

To Daniel

Acknowledgement

This dissertation is the result of an inspiring time at the Department of Economics and Business Administration at the Goethe University Frankfurt. The thesis could have not been completed without the support from my advisors, colleagues, friends, and family.

First and foremost, I am deeply indebted to my supervisor, Roland Eisen, for his encouraging support, his guidance, and countless invaluable suggestions. My work benefited tremendously from his advice. Many thanks also go to my second supervisor, Bernd Fitzenberger.

I am grateful to my colleagues Wolfgang Strengmann-Kuhn, Marko Susnik, and Florian Täube at the Goethe University Frankfurt. In particular, I sincerely appreciate the motivating exchange with my partner Daniel and his family as well as with my friends Dunja, Natalie, Loli, and Filiz.

Finally, I would like to thank my wonderful family, the family of my partner, and my partner Daniel for their loving support throughout my years of education, their dedication, and their understanding during the time I worked on the dissertation. I cannot quite articulate how much I owe to all of them.

Abstract

In the focus of the health care market analyses usually are the continually increasing health care expenditures (HCE) and their future development. Considering these increasing HCE, price regulation measures are applied in the relevant pharmaceutical market to contain this increase. Some at least in the past of this believe that HCE mainly rise due to medico-technical and pharmaceutical innovation and ageing. The dissertation discusses these ideas. It consists of three papers and a concluding summary. The first one concerns international measures of price regulation and their consequences. The two following essays analyze the empirical relationship between pharmaceutical innovation and ageing. The main conclusions are: the ageing effect causes rising expenditures on pharmaceuticals as well as increasing pharmaceutical innovations instrumented either as patent applications or new drug approvals; the R&D expenditures of the pharmaceutical industry lead to rising expenditures on pharmaceuticals but decreasing overall HCE; additionally, decreasing mortality is found to increase HCE. These results do not support the medicalisation hypothesis of a disproportional increase of HCE with rising share of elderly. Therefore, the overall impact of pharmaceutical progress on HCE is not clear-cut. There are evidences that higher medical costs reduce overall HCE. Consequently predominating conclusions and political implications should be reconsidered.

Contents

List of Tables

List of Figures

Chapter 1

Introduction

In the focus of the health care market analyzes usually lay the continually increasing health care expenditures (HCE) and their future development. Therefore, the starting point for my dissertation are the increasing health care expenditures. As expenditures on pharmaceuticals have grown faster than any other major component of HCE since the late 1990s, I particularly focus on the pharmaceutical markets. The aim is to scrutinize the pattern of expenditure and the different governments' cost containment interventions. Based upon these previous considerations concerning the pricing policies for the pharmaceutical market, in the following analyses I specifically emphasise the identification of relevant factors influencing the health care spending such as ageing and pharmaceutical innovation.

Chapter 2 (Eisen and Ilgin (2007)) presents a detailed picture of the international pricing policies applied in the pharmaceutical market.
Governmental price regulation of drugs has become a popular measure to control health care spending. This development revives the questions whether and if so how these regulation measures are accomplishing the goal to control drug spending. According to the different interest groups the answers will be different. It is time that governments with their health insurance or health care systems face rising health care expenditures, especially expenditures on drugs. In attempts to contain the expenditures for drugs or other health care services, different countries took various regulation strategies. To compare the effects due to different pricing policies for pharmaceutical markets the national intervention are examined and evaluated.

In recent literature it is often argued that the government should try to set the price ceiling of drugs low in order to reduce public health expenditures. However, setting the price ceiling of drugs low leads to a reduction of incentives for innovation or even an off-shoring of the production of pharmaceutical companies. The modern medical science has particularly been progressive with biotechnological medical acquisitions on one side, but the very same acquisition is quoted in the literature to be one of the reasons for 'cost explosion' in health care systems. According to Krämer (1996), technical progress itself creates needs, which exist at the most concealed, i.e. technical progress is the greatest cost driver itself. Besides new technologies, demographic patterns, market imperfections, the method and length of regulatory approval, inadequate product differentiation for the same medical indication category, and brand loyalty can be identified as crucial factors for rising pharmaceutical expenditures.

Market failures are caused by supply side entry barriers, e.g. patents, by agency relationships, and by moral hazard. Due to the occurring moral hazard in the prescribing process, it is not sure whether competition alone could guarantee efficient prices.

The aim of our research is to evaluate the effectiveness of selected demand and supply side measures, keeping in mind crucial factors in this market, for instance the free rider problem and moral hazard. On account of the international expansion of the pharmaceutical market and the globalization of the drug industry, multinational economic evaluation is an important aspect in public policy and corporate decisions. Nevertheless, only few multinational economic evaluations have been made due to the fact of missing comparable data.

Therefore, in order to draw a qualitative multinational comparison, a review of the different existing national price regulation schemes is necessary. Patents' regulations and parallel imports as supply side price regulation measures, and drug budgets for physicians, generic drugs and reference price limits on reimbursement as demand side price regulation measures will be reviewed.

To analyze reference price limits on reimbursement, a small static two class product model is introduced. By using a sequential price-setting process within the model it can be shown that, applying marginal cost pricing for drugs clustered within Phase 1, welfare can be increased. If government sets the reference price equal to the marginal costs, welfare can be increased without free riding on the sunk R&D costs of researching pharmaceutical firms because the patent protection has expired.

To give a comprehensive evaluation of the other pricing policies, the interactions between regulative measures are taken into account. In the past too many regulative measures to contain health care expenditures have been targeted primarily to the supply side or to the demand side. But, regulation that only applies on one side of the market does little to control the rising expenditures. Without simultaneous use of demand side incentives and volume controls, pharmaceutical expenditures probably can not be reduced effectively.

Chapter 3 (Ilgin and Eisen (2007)) focuses on the link between health care expenditures and expenditures on prescribed drugs and demographic change and pharmaceutical innovations.

Several studies forecasting health care spending predict continuously increasing expenses due to at least three different factors: ageing, technical progress, and increasing prices. Depending on different arguments demographical change and medical progress can be seen as reciprocate boosting or extenuating factors on health care expenditures.

Medical progress connected to a healthier way of living can lead to a reduction of proximity to death interval and therefore to a decline of ageing related HCE in the corresponding cohorts. The over-all effect due to the medical progress could be a decrease of HCE for an ageing population.

The aim of this study is to identify the effects of important influencing factors on the expenditures of prescribed drugs (EPD) and OTC drugs (EOD), e.g. the share of 65 aged and older (henceforth: the share of 65+), doctors' consultations, and R&D expenditures of pharmaceutical industry. As EPD have grown faster than any other major component of HCE since the late 1990s, cross-national differences in pharmaceutical expenditures are of great interest. Taking into account the potential push factors for pharmaceutical innovation production, we also incorporate as additional factors the rest life expectancy at age 65 and the R&D expenditures of pharmaceutical industry to estimate pharmaceutical innovations instrumented as patent applications.

With panel data of seven countries (Australia, Canada, Finland, France, Germany, Japan and US) from 1991 to 2001 a within group estimator and a dynamic panel estimator, namely the first-differenced General Method of Moments (GMM), have been applied to test the following hypotheses: 1) if the share of 65+, doctors' consultations, and R&D expenditures of pharmaceutical industry increase, then HCE and EPD will increase. 2) If the rest life expectancy at age 65 as well as R&D expenditures of pharmaceutical industry increase, then innovations instrumented as patent applications will increase; but the share of 65+ as well as the doctors' consultations and R&D expenditures of pharmaceutical industry are not expected to determine total EOD.

In our panel analysis it can be shown that, in contrast to effects in health care expenditures in other studies, there is an ageing effect (pull factor) causing rising EPD as well as for innovations instrumented as patent applications inter alia for pharmaceuticals. Thus, an increasing population of 65 years and over leads to rising EPD, and increasing further life expectancy at age 65 leads to rising patent applications. Additionally, we found a push factor, namely R&D expenditures of pharmaceutical industry causing rising EPD but decreasing HCE and increasing innovations. And finally increasing doctors' consultations per capita reduce EPD. This indicates that the moral hazard behaviour in prescribing drugs can not be confirmed. Probably only control with check-up examination without drug prescription are applied. Increasing doctors' consultations may lead to decreasing EPD because of successful application of lower medical therapies or by additional following-up therapies without drug applications which are not affecting EPD.

Chapter 4 (Ilgin (2007)) turns toward the German health care market and examines the effects of mortality and new drug approvals for the public health care expenditures.

In the previous chapter we analyzed the effects between ageing and pharmaceutical innovation from an international perspective, here the national perspective comes to the fore supplemented with a short forecast. Several studies forecasting health care spending predict continuously increasing expenses. The aim of this study is to identify the effects of relevant factors for the German public health care expenditures (PHCE).

Using a vector autoregressive model (VAR) including data from Germany for a period of 19 years (1986-2004), it can be shown that the current German public health care expenditures are influenced by PHCE of previous periods, potential years of life lost, and the approval of new drugs by the German Federal Institute for Drugs and Medical Devices.

Results show that potential years of life lost decrease with increasing PHCE and increasing new drug approvals. Whereas the PHCE rise with increasing new drug approvals and high lagged PHCE and rising potential years of life lost. As already shown in previous studies in fact there are structural factors causing continuously rising PHCE but also causing continuously decreasing potential years of life lost. The continuous decrease of potential years of life lost and increase of further life expectancy at age 65 can be interpreted as indicators of overall health improvements.

Translating these developments into concrete gains in economic output could result in an increase of worker productivity. A greater workforce not only enlarges the pool of available labour yielding to a potential improvement of productivity but also to lower labour costs.

Chapter 5 sums up previous empirical results and based upon these results conclusions are drawn and political implications are elaborated.

Some argue that HCE mainly rise due to medico-technical and pharmaceutical innovation and ageing. Previous studies examine the relation between innovation and ageing. The main conclusions are: the ageing effect causes rising expenditures on pharmaceuticals as well as increasing pharmaceutical innovations instrumented either as patent applications or new drug approvals; the R&D expenditures of the pharmaceutical industry lead to rising expenditures on pharmaceuticals but decreasing overall HCE; additionally, decreasing mortality is found to increase HCE. These results do not support the medicalisation hypothesis of a disproportional increase of HCE with rising share of elderly. Therefore, the overall impact of pharmaceutical progress on HCE is not clear-cut. There are evidences that these higher medical costs reduce overall HCE. Consequently predominating conclusions and political implications are reconsidered in this chapter.

Chapter 2

Price Regulations in the Pharmaceutical Market - An International Perspective

1. Introduction

Why should government intervene in pricing of pharmaceutical firms? Or should they intervene at all? To answer these questions one could start with the classical distinction between supply and demand side of pharmaceutical market. According to the different interest groups the answers will be different. Fact is that most governments face rising health care expenditures, especially expenditures on drugs (Figure 2.1). In attempts to contain the expenditures for drugs or other health care services, different countries took various regulation strategies.

The modern medical science has particularly been progressive with biotechnological medical acquisitions on one side, but the very same acquisition is quoted in literature to be one of the reason for cost explosion in health care systems. Technical progress itself creates needs, which exist at the most concealed, i.e. technical progress is the greatest cost driver itself (Krämer (1996)). Besides new technologies, demographic patterns, market imperfections, the method and length of regulatory approval, inadequate product differentiation for the same medical indication category, and brand loyalty can be identified as crucial factors for rising pharmaceutical expenditures. Market failures are caused by supply side entry barriers, e.g. patents, by agency relationships, and by moral hazard. Moral hazard occurs because of the specific demand structure comprised of four segments: the physicians who prescribe the pharmaceuticals, the pharmacists who dispense them, the patients who consume, and governments or insurers who pay. Due to the occurring moral hazard in this prescribing process, it is not secured that competition alone could guarantee efficient prices (Mrazek (2002)).

Figure 2.1: Share of drug spending of the total health care spending in Europe, Japan and USA (1991 and 2001*)

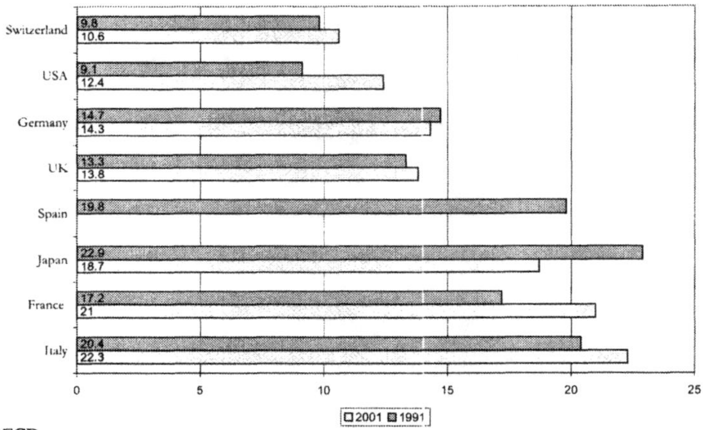

Source: OECD

* Germany 1992 (for 1991), Spain 1990 (only available value) und UK 2002 (for 2001).

On account of the international expansion of the pharmaceutical market and the globalization of the drug industry, multinational economic evaluation is an important aspect in public policy and corporate decisions. Nevertheless, only few multinational economic evaluations have been made due to the fact of missing comparable data. Therefore, in order to draw a qualitative multinational comparison a review of the different existing national price regulation schemes is necessary.

The paper is organized as follows. In the first section an overview of the current situation in the health care market and several developments in the pharmaceutical market will be given. In the second section important aspect for the pharmaceutical pricing are touched on as for example the free-rider problem, moral hazard, and also the cost structure of drugs in general. The objective is to illustrate current problems of the production of pharmaceuticals. The main and third section of this paper contributes to the price regulation, in particular the aims of price regulation and the various types of national price regulations. At the end an evaluation is given. The different implications and conclusions will be discussed in the last section.

2. Crucial Factors in Pharmaceutical Pricing

2.1. Free-rider Problem and Moral Hazard

In the recent literature opinions do not differ in the point that first nations have incentives to free ride on the enormous sunk costs of pharmaceutical firms (PHs), and try to apply the marginal cost pricing in order to maximize the welfare. For the social insurance systems this means that governments, as a monopsony buyer for pharmaceuticals, has strong vested interest to concentrate on the short-run interests of containing the own pharmaceutical budget implying that the own measures are negligible on the manufactures' incentives for R&D that result out of their global earnings. Hence, each country has an incentive to successively reduce the prices up to the marginal costs while ignoring global joint costs (Danzon (1997b)).

Second, nations have also incentives to support pharmaceutical firms with respect to their innovation costs by granting them monopoly rights by means of patents for example. Therefore the firms can ask an adequately high mark-up on the marginal cost.[1] But at least nations try to secure a certain research and development (R&D) level, because anticipating this free-rider problem a drastic reaction by pharmaceutical firms may be the decision not to invest in R&D at all (Danzon (1997b)). The production sector of pharmaceuticals is also an important growth sector in many industrialized countries. Thus, besides health care spending government has to consider also consequences for employment. Therefore, nations are faced with a dilemma. Furthermore the producers of generics as suppliers of unpatented drugs are interested in the research findings of these pharmaceutical firms. Using the information of expired patents puts producers of generics into the position to utilize dearly researched coherences for their production. Therefore, they free-ride on the sunk R&D costs of the researching firms.

Figure 2.2 shows that German manufacturers are obtaining the lowest and Sweden manufacturers are obtaining the highest share in the breakdown of final retailed prices. Beside Ireland and

[1] According to Danzon (1997b) marginal cost pricing would only cover 30% or less of the total cost.

the Netherlands no country allows the wholesalers 10% or more. On average the pharmacists get the second highest share. Also the taxation is rather differently treated.

Figure 2.2: Breakdown of the final price for retailed pharmaceuticals (2002), in percent

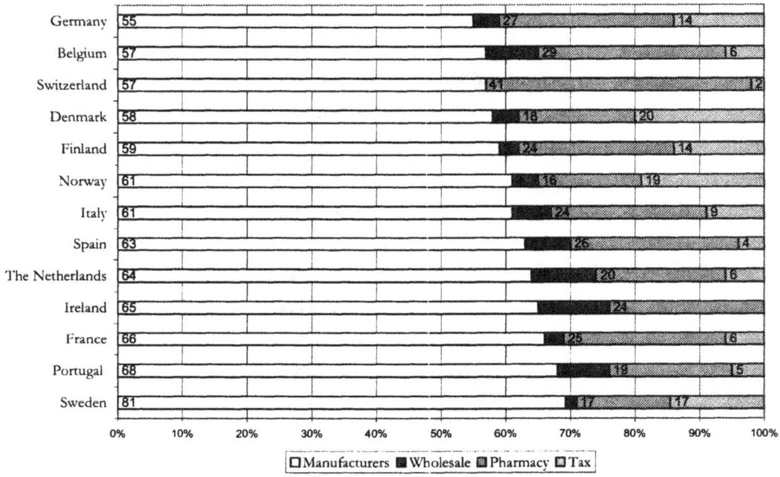

Source: VFA (2004), p.19.

Beside the free-rider problem, also a moral hazard can emerge, in particular, on the side of physicians. Physicians for example tend to prescribe more pharmaceuticals than necessary to commit the patients on themselves. Consequently, the amount of prescriptions are rising and this in turn causes rising expenditures in health care spending. Furthermore, moral hazard exists on the patients' side in the form of excessive consuming. Patients try to hoard as many medicaments as possible aiming at compensating for their insurance payment.

2.2. Cost Structure of Drugs

R&D costs account for 30% of total costs because the drug development process is risky, time-consuming and heavily regulated. These global joint costs are necessary to develop and in

the end to bring the drug to the market, i.e. they can not be properly classified as belonging to any individual drug. Additionally, these costs are sunk at the point of price fixing or price negotiations (Danzon (1997a)). Furthermore, the ratio between sunk costs (sc) and marginal costs (mc) increases over the life time of a pharmaceutical.
This can lead firstly to types of regulation that are reducing incentives for innovative R&D and pushing towards copying R&D or secondly to types of regulation which benefit pharmaceutical firms in the home country. Still, it is a challenge for national policy to create a system that mediates between curbing down the health care expenditures and providing sufficient incentives for innovative R&D leading to optimal health care.
Patents for example can be such a mediator to promote innovations. Patent rights secure the innovator or innovative firm a price above the marginal cost for the life time of the patent as long as the patent prevents competition from close substitutes (Danzon (1997a)).

3. Price Regulations

3.1. Objectives of Price Regulations

First and foremost the aim of price regulation is to control rising health care expenditures. Health care payers can either concentrate on the demand (volume) or the supply (price) or on both sides. As mentioned above the second aim of price regulation in the pharmaceutical market is to support industrial policy goals of home investment, employment, and international competitiveness. Italy or France for example allow higher prices for pharmaceuticals if they are produced in the home country. In the U.K. the rate of return on capital within the country is the crucial factor. In this way domestic investment is promoted but these kind of regulations could also distort productive efficiency (Danzon (1997a)).
As the drug costs become a gradually increasing element of the health care spending, economic evaluations can be used to inform governments and health care organizations to supplement clinical evidence on safety and efficacy. This information can be used for reimbursement negotiations, resource management, and temporary regulation and price control (Smith (2002)).
Figure 2.3 shows a possible division of demand and supply side measures. In the following subsections some of these demand and supply side measures are discussed and evaluated.

Figure 2.3: Regulatory framework for pharmaceutical markets

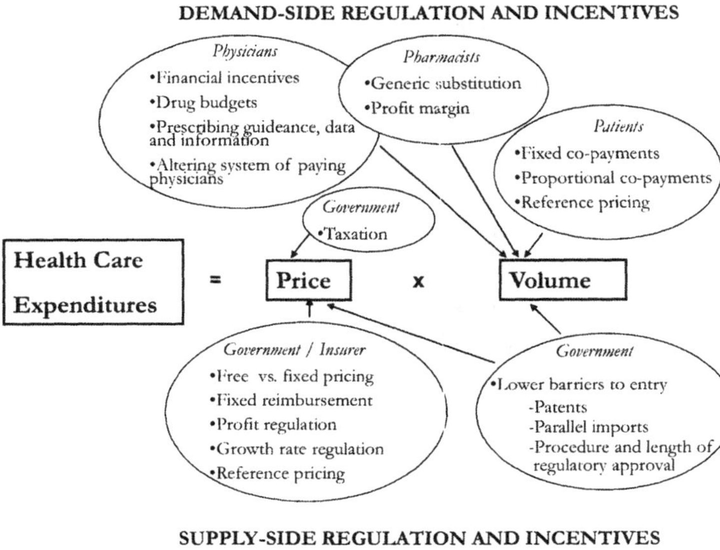

Source: Mrazek (2002), p. 455 and author's own compilation

These regulation schemes include certain norms that have to be fulfilled by existing drugs. Government have different views with regard to the strictness of these regulations. The USA started with the Pure Food and Drug Act of 1906. For a certain period the United States had the most strict drug testing prerequisites in the world, but today the United Kingdom and Germany have caught up (Scherer (2000)).

A new European system for approval of new drug has come into effect in January 1995. It offers two ways to approve medical products. One way is a more 'centralized' form, which has been implemented by creating the European Medical Products Evaluation Agency (EMEA). The second is a 'mutual acknowledgement' procedure in the EU member states selected by the applicant and then by mutual acknowledgement of national market approval.[2] Through this European reform a platform of introducing new drugs has been created.

The decision-makers' problem is to find the best solution between making a Type I error of supporting a drug which is not truly safe or effective and a Type II error of withholding a drug

[2]For detailed information see Regulation 2309/936 and Directive 93/41/EEC.

which is truly effective and safe. Intuitively comprehensible, governments are particularly concerned not to commit Type I errors, to avoid political disasters caused by pharmaceuticals that lead for example to cancer or malformed babies. To reduce this risk, the size of necessary clinical trials has been increased and also the availability of new drugs has been retarded (Scherer (2000)).

3.2. Types of Supply-Side Price Regulations

3.2.1. Reference Price Limits on Reimbursement

Reference pricing is a basic concept. Drugs are classified into clusters according to particular criteria or rather the degrees of similar therapeutic effects. Government or the insurer determines a reference price for each cluster on the basis of a relative lower priced drug within the cluster (Danzon and Ketcham (2003)). Figure 2.4 shows the share of drugs which are comprised of reference price limits in Germany.

Figure 2.4: Share of reference price limits in Germany (2000-2003*)

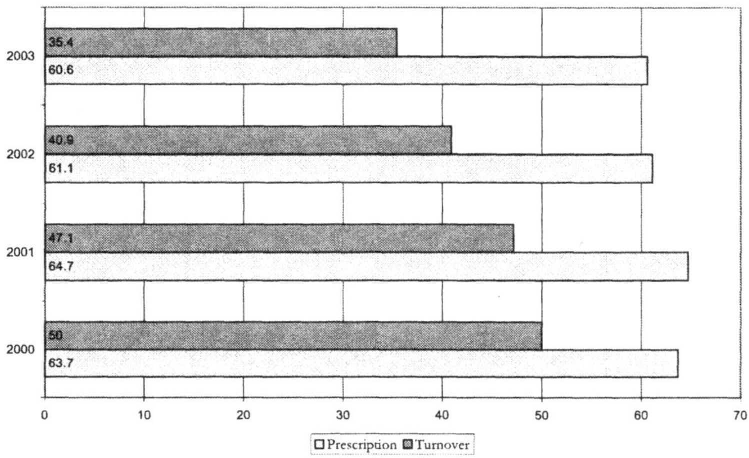

Source: VFA (2004), p.63

* Values are taken on January 1st each year and 2003 are preliminary values.

Germany was the first country to introduce reference pricing in 1989 together with the Health Reform Law ('Gesundheitsreform-Gesetz (GRG)'). The aim of this law was to induce more intensive competition in order to contain drug expenses.[3] Reference price reimbursement systems have been also launched in Denmark, New Zealand, and Canada.

Reference price limits usually have been established using a two-step procedure. In the first step it is defined which drugs can be clustered. These clustered drugs may be described by the same chemical entity (or molecular entity),[4] or with comparable therapeutic effects.[5] This clustering guarantees that the therapeutical possibilities have not been restricted, and therefore physicians have the opportunity to prescribe alternative compounds. In the second step the prevailing reference price limit is determined. Here, the price have to fulfil certain criteria, e.g. to guarantee a sufficient, suitable, economic and quality enhancing medical care (BGA (2004)). The patients have to carry the cost above the reimbursement price in Germany; physicians are obliged by law to point out this fact. The price elasticity is much higher if patients have to pay this difference by themselves, therefore manufacturers tend to adapt to the reference prices (Danzon (1997a)).

3.2.2. Patents and Parallel Imports

The idiosyncratic subject matter of patents is to guarantee the holder the exclusive right to use his invention with regards to produce industrial products and putting them into circulation for the first time. This can be done by the patent holder either directly or by granting licenses to third parties. The aim of patents is to reward the creative effort of the invention.

In the European Union the patent protection lasts for 20 years and normally assigns the power to discriminate prices between countries. The cost structure of pharmaceuticals is character-

[3]The reference price limits on reimbursement regulation applies on the demand and supply side of the pharmaceutical market. The demand side is affected because patients do not receive full reimbursement for the pharmaceuticals whose prices are higher. The supply-side is concerned because of increased price competition.

[4]The distinction between chemical entities (CE) and molecular entities (ME) is small. CE are new molecules or compounds not tested in human before. ME is used to describe compounds.

[5]In Phase 1 of the German system and also most of the Medicaid programs in USA usually generically equivalent products and drugs, where the patent rights have been lost, are clustered in the same group. Phase 2 includes clustering of drugs with related chemicals, for example Benzodiazepines or H2 antagonists. In Phase 3 also drugs with therapeutic comparable effects are grouped together.

ized by high R&D sunk costs.[6] One basic aspect of this share of the global joint costs is that they are constant independent of the number of future consumers or countries that will use the drug. Obviously, R&D and the resulting inapplicability of marginal cost pricing is not only a problem for the pharmaceutical market. The goal of patent protection is to find a solution for this problem. This normally enables the patent holder to price discriminate between countries, primarily because the holder enjoys in each country unregulated distribution rights, including parallel imports (European Commission (2003a)).

The European Court of Justice can constrain the manufacturer's patent rights by decreeding the patent holders rights. The patent holders rights are exhausted throughout the EU once a product has been placed on the market in any EU country. The effect is to nullify the patent holder's rights in the importing country (Danzon (1997b)).[7]

The value of patent protection is further bounded in most European countries by price regulation and other forms of regulation because of the government's role of insurer. In Europe, different governments have important functions, either as a monopoly provider of national health insurance, as e.g. in UK or Italy, or as regulator of the social insurance health funds, as e.g. in Germany, France or the Netherlands (Danzon (1997b)).

The limitations of the patent protection have significantly influenced the decisions concerning parallel imports or trade. The European Commission defines parallel trade as trade in products which takes place outside the official distribution system established by a particular firm. The own distribution system of the firm may cause differences in prices for different countries, utilizing national differences in the behavior of consumers (price discrimination). Parallel traders buy products in countries where they are sold at lower prices caused e.g. by price regulation and sell them in high-price countries with less or no interventions. The flow of products thereby created is called parallel trade (European Commission (2003b)).

In principal parallel imports are about goods or property rights on goods which are traded beside and therefore parallel to a contractually agreed distribution network. Parallel imports come

[6] DiMasi, Hansen, and Grabowski (2003) find that the total R&D costs per new drug is about US$ 802 million in 2000 dollars. A critical assessment is given by Frank (2003).

[7] For details see judgements of the European Court of Justice: Merck vs Primecrown C-267 and C-268/95 (1996) ECR I-6285. Parallel imports of pharmaceuticals is a lawful kind of trade within the Internal Market based on article 28 of the Treaty and subject to the impairment in view of the protection of human health and life and the protection of industrial and commercial property, regulated in article 30 of the Treaty. The European Court of Justice defines the European Union as a single market consisting of different European countries.

into a country not by the producers' intentionally designated ways of selected sales dealers or single importers etc. Reimports however are goods exported from the home country to foreign countries and which are imported back to the home country (Freytag (2001), p. 17).

Legalization of parallel imports implies a decision with respect to the possible form of price discrimination. On the one side, the possibility to discriminate prices is restricted, because the producers can not sell unaffected any longer the same goods for different prices. On the other side, parallel imports are only possible because of intercountry price differences (Goate, Rhys, and Gerner (1999)). But these intercountry differences are usually based upon national pricing policies and different national interests. Supposing that parallel trade operates as an important stimulating force for market integration where there are given price differences between Member States, it is only one kind of importing national pricing policies. If an European harmonized pricing policy for pharmaceuticals would exist parallel import could not exist. But harmonization of the European pricing policies can not be a goal if there are different national costs and different national interests.[8]

Recent literature points out that governments have a rational motivation to free ride on the sunk costs of innovative pharmaceutical firms. Thus, the question is whether this free-rider problem can be solved by parallel imports. The health expenditures can be reduced by setting the drug price ceiling as low as possible. Before a new drug can be brought onto the market high investments are necessary. The problem with these investments is that they are already sunk cost when national drug price ceilings are determined. Within a static perspective sunk costs are not taken into account when deciding on the optimal price. However, these sunk costs amount to 30% of the total costs (Danzon (1997b)). Providing them patents seems to be a rational procedure, because pharmaceutical firm incur high costs in developing new drugs: One major cost driver are R&D expenditures to cover investigations in compounds that have been dropped (so called 'dry holes'). The other major cost driver are the tied up capital costs, because the process to invent and to bring NCE to market takes at least one decade.[9]

[8]Maybe parallel imports could be seen in sense of a Pareto optimizing game. An outcome of a game is Pareto optimal if there is no other outcome that makes every player at least as well off and at least one player strictly better off. To describe the existing situation with a Pareto optimal outcome is inadequate, because the price discrimination of the patent holder is worse off and the volume of sales that are not parallel imported goods decreases.

[9]See DiMasi, Hansen, and Grabowski (2003) for the difference between average out-of-the pocket costs of an new chemical entity (NCE) and the average cost of an NCE (including capital costs): 403-802$. But these costs reflect the outcomes of profit-maximizing choices and are not useful parameters to evaluate the value of an

Figure 2.5: Savings by reimportation in different European countries (2002)

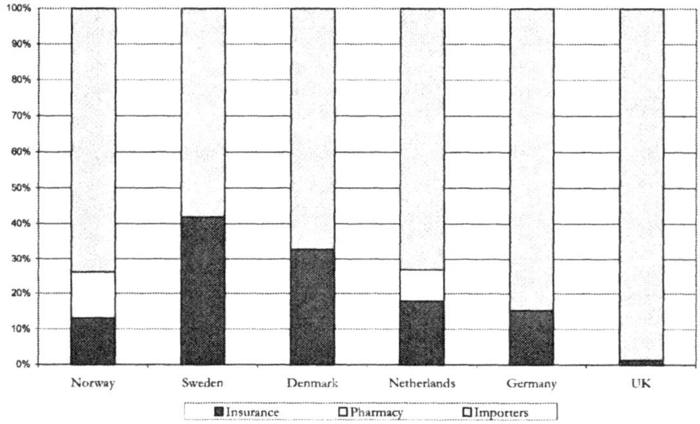

Source: IMS Health Data. For detailed information see Kanavos, Costa-i Font, Merkur, and Gemmill (2003)

Figure 2.5 shows the savings in different European countries that could be made by reimportation. These date have been presented together with a stakeholder analysis by Kanavos, Costa-i Font, Merkur, and Gemmill (2003) which aims at examining the impact of parallel imports. They demonstrate that the profits from parallel imports flow for the most part to third-party firms that buy and resell patented pharmaceuticals.

3.3. Types of Demand-Side Price Regulations

3.3.1. Drug Budget Regulations for Physicians

There are three categories of regulations to influence the prescribing behavior of physicians. The most basic category is the restriction of potentially prescribable drugs by introducing so called positive[10] or negative lists[11]. The second more general possibility is to give compre-

investment.

[10]A positive list is a compilation of in principal permitted drugs which are provided within the scope of health care insurance systems and therefore the costs are reimbursed. Patients have to pay for drugs that are not listed.

[11]A negative list is a compilation of drugs where the prescription at the expense of the statutory health insurance funds is not permitted.

hensive guidelines, which are mainly based on therapeutic considerations, and monitoring of prescribing practices. The guidelines stipulate which drugs can be prescribed and in some countries they even specify how prescriptions are written. The third category, drug budget regulation for physicians, includes measures to provide incentives for physicians to consider cost differences between alternative treatments.

Probably one of the most powerful demand side measures to regulate drug spending is to place physicians directly at risk for the financial consequences of their prescribing practice (Danzon (1997a)). It is often argued, that physicians do not directly benefit from prescribing drugs but indirectly be securing repeated visits by patients.

Table 2.1: Development of physician drug budgets with individual and collective liability in Germany (1989-2003)

	Spending caps (collective liability)	**Target volumes (collective liability)**
1989 to 1992	No spending caps required	Target volumes legally required but not implemented due to lack of data
1993	Legally set national spending caps	
1994 to 1997	Negotiated regional spending caps	
1998	No spending caps required	Negotiated target volumes for individual practices (lack of legal liability)
1999	Legally set national spending caps	
2000 to 2001	Negotiated regional spending caps	
Since 2002	No spending caps	Legal liability for negotiated target volumes for individual practices

Source: Schreyögg and Busse (2004), p.5

(The darker the shading, the more strictly the regulation is.)

After launching drug budgets in Germany in 1993 two different types containing varying degrees of governmental regulation have been used. On the one hand, spending caps for all physicians of a region were defined, putting all of them into responsibility for any excess of the region's aggregated drug budget. On the other hand, target volumes for individual classes of physicians were defined (Schreyögg and Busse (2004)).

The chronology of the physicians' drug budgets is shown in Table 2.1. As it became clear that collective liability was not very successful target caps with individual liability were introduced in 1998. These target volumes were accompanied by an early information system given to the physicians. Since 2000 each physician receives information about the aggregate prescription volume of his specialist class in his region and about his own prescription volume. In 2002 the liability for negotiated target volumes for individual practices have been statutory determined. The statutory cap for overstepping and repaying is 125% over the individual target (§106(5a) German Social Law, SGB V).

3.3.2. Generic drugs

After a regular patent duration of 20 years and loss of patent rights, producer of generic drugs (imitation) can be admitted into this part of the drug market. The share of the generic drugs is around 70% of the prescriptions of the German health insurance funds. In the last 12 years a clear trend towards prescribing generics appears. This tendency to prescribe more generics can be seen in the increasing share of prescribed generics as a percentage of the total prescriptions. Often enough pharmaceutical firms with patent protected drugs loose considerable market share within a few months.

Just after the introduction of drug budgets in Germany the market share of generics increased by 3.7% in 1993 and in the following by 1.3% each year. In 2002 the market share of generic prescriptions exceeded the market share of original compounds (see Figure 2.6).

In 2002, a scheme for generic substitution has been launched in Germany. Under the well known 'aut-idem regulation' pharmacists are asked to substitute non-patented pharmaceuticals above a certain reference price limit by other compounds. Physicians still have the possibility to avoid this by explicitly indicating on the prescription that they do not want the pharmacists to substitute the drugs. The effect of the aut-idem regulation was not strong and therefore canceled at the end of 2003, but it should be kept in mind while interpreting the data (Schreyögg and Busse (2004)).

Figure 2.6: Market share of generic versus original prescriptions in the German Statutory Health Insurance scheme

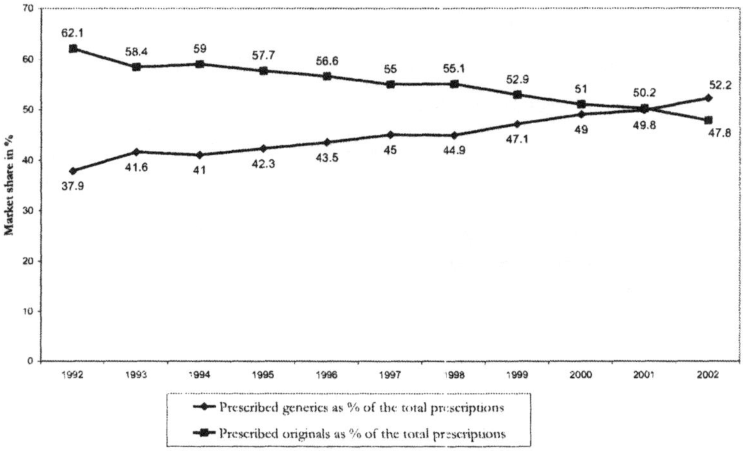

Source: Research Institute of general regional sickness funds (WIdO)

4. Evaluation of Price Regulations

4.1. Evaluation of Supply-Side Types

4.1.1. Reference Price Limits on Reimbursement

Following the simple two country model of Königbauer (2004) explaining the effects of parallel imports a static two class product model will be introduced in order to analyze reference pricing.[12] Using a sequential price-setting process it can be shown that, applying marginal cost pricing for drugs clustered within Phase 1, welfare can be increased.

Researching pharmaceutical companies produce patent protected drugs i in the home country H. Beside researching companies generic drug producing companies exist. The researching companies are confronted with large sunk R&D costs RD and marginal costs c. The generic

[12] In this static consideration the sunk R&D costs have no effect for the optimal price regulation.

drug producing companies manufacture generic drugs j and are only confronted with the average costs of production which are assumed to correspond to the marginal costs c. The drugs i and j can be freely traded with a corresponding market approval. Demand for patent protected drugs in unregulated markets is $q_i(p_i)$, $i = 1,...,n$. Demand of generic drugs in unregulated markets is $q_j(p_j)$, $j = 1,...,m$. Demand of patent protected and generic drugs in markets with reference price limits depends on current reference prices of a certain cluster. The structure of the model is as follows.

In the first stage, the firm decides whether or not to be in the market regulated by reference price limits of reimbursement. The decision depends on the resulting profits. The resulting profits have to be at least as high as the launching costs of the drug. If the expected profit is too low the firm will not be in the market. The researching pharmaceutical company will set a price above or equal to the reference price, therefore the patent rights expired drug price is as follows $p_i \geq p_{rp}$.[13]

In the second stage, the government sets a reference price p_{rp} which determines the maximum reimbursable price.[14] The optimal reference price p^*_{rp} maximizing welfare in home country H where welfare is composed of consumer surplus $S_H(p_{rp}) = \int_{p_{rp}}^{q^{-1}(0)} q_{rp}(p)dp$, the researching pharmaceutical firm's profit in the unregulated market is $\pi_i(p_i) = (p_i - c)q_i(p_i)$, and the generic producing pharmaceutical firm's profit in the unregulated market is $\pi_j(p_j) = (p_j - c)q_j(p_j)$:

$$max \quad S_H(p_{rp}) + \pi_i(p_i) + \pi_j(p_j) \tag{2.1}$$

In the third stage, the generic producing pharmaceutical firm sets a price below or equal to the reference price, therefore the generic drug price is as follows $p_j \leq p_{rp}$.[15] It can be assumed that the researching pharmaceutical firm and the generic drug producing firm will set prices as

[13] Caves, Whinston, and Hurwitz (1991) analyzed price effects that followed patent expiration and subsequent entry of generic drugs from 1976 to 1987. They found that brand-name drug prices decreased by 4.5% following the entry of generic drugs into previously uncontested markets. But these effects were not significantly different from zero.

[14] In Phase 1 government will set the reference price equal to the marginal costs c because Phase 1 contains cluster with generically equivalent drugs, where the patent rights have been expired.

[15] The assumptions that generic drug producer price is equal or below and researching pharmaceutical firms price is equal or above the reference price are reasonable. Caves, Whinston, and Hurwitz (1991) state that generic drugs tend to enter into the market at whole sale prices 40 to 70 percent of those prevailing before the original drug's patent expired.

near as possible or equal to the current reference price. The researching pharmaceutical firm will also lower its prices for the patent rights expired drug in order not to loose market shares but will still set the price above the reference price hoping that a certain reputation and brand loyalty will secure a consumer commitment to pay the corresponding co-payment.[16] It can be shown that if in home country the prices will be set approximately equal to marginal cost the reference price will correspond to the marginal costs.[17]

$$\frac{d[S_H(p_{rp}) + \pi_i(p_{rp}) + \pi_j(p_{rp})]}{dp_{rp}} = -q_{rp}(p_{rp}) + q_{rp}(p_{rp}) + (p_{rp} - c)q'_{rp}(p_{rp}) = 0$$

$$\Rightarrow p^*_{rp} = c \qquad (2.2)$$

Due to resulting reference price the generic drug producer will also set the prices equal to the reference price and generic drug price is as follows, $p_j = c = p_{rp}$.

By setting the reference price equal to the marginal costs welfare can be increased without free riding on the sunk R&D cost of the researching firm because the patent protection has expired. As generic drugs tend to enter into the market at whole sale price of 40 to 70 percent of those prevailing before the patent protection expired, the question can be asked, why generic drug competition is not stronger, considering that generic drug producers have no R&D costs.

Figure 2.7 shows the price development of drugs which are clustered within the reference pricing. Drugs are clustered accordingly to the two step procedure of reference price limits in Phase 1 and Phase 2. With the introduction of the Statutory Health Insurance Modernization Law ('GKV Modernisierungsgesetz (GMG)') in January 2004 a modified drug prescribing enactment has been established. This usually causes a reduction of prescribing higher priced drugs and an increase of drugs which are fully reimbursed within the reference price limits. The change of the indices between the actual period and prior periods are not comparable if new reference priced drugs have been introduced into the market. In the sub-markets the actual market share have been considered, this means the change of the indices is based on current market conditions.

[16]The accepted price difference between the reference price and the price of the out of patent drug that will be paid depends on the price elasticity of demand.

[17]This procedure causes no free rider problem because reference pricing in Phase 1 includes only drugs where the patent rights have been expired.

Figure 2.7: Price indices according to different market segments (January 2003 to January 2005)

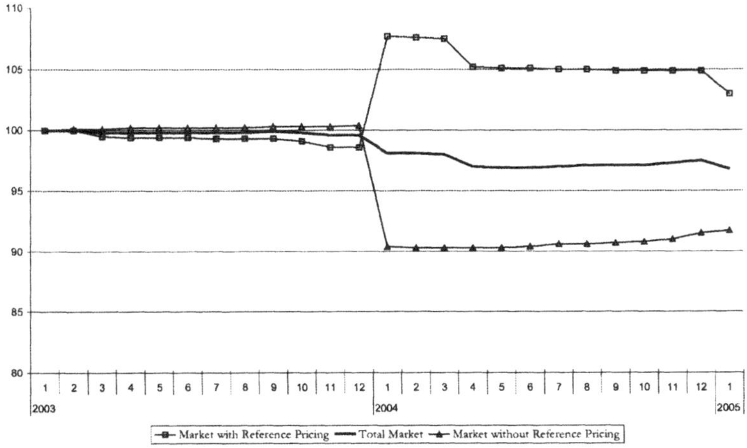

Source: Nink (2005), p.10

The main advantage of reference price limits on reimbursement lies in the enhanced competition between products within a certain cluster. A disadvantage is that the competition below the reference price is reduced or rather completely eliminated. In unrestricted industries, manufacturers have to all intents and purposes an incentive to reduce prices if demand is elastic so that a price reduction creates an equivalent increase in volume. But in the German pharmaceutical market the demand is still rather inelastic at prices below the reference price. However, demand is elastic at prices above the reference prices but only between the range of the corresponding co-payments.

Prior experiences in Germany and other countries with reference price limits on reimbursement showed that patients have a high price elasticity for pharmaceuticals with co-payments and are therefore strongly interested to avoid co-payments. Thus, reference pricing as a demand side regulation is efficient and introduces an effective measure to influence the volume of demand for pharmaceuticals. As consequence pharmaceutical producers have to adapt their pricing to reference limits if their products are clustered in order to prevent a loss of market share (IMS Health (2004)). An essential feature is that the results are different according to the particular assumptions made regarding the availability of information to the potential buyer and their response to it (Lu and Comanor (1998)). Lu and Comanor (1998) found pharmaceutical pricing behavior is a mixture of skimming and penetration strategies[18]: if pharmaceutical firms are launching a significant innovation they will use the skimming strategy and if me-too products are introduced the penetration strategy will be used. Obviously, with the introduction of a reference price limit on reimbursement the use of penetration strategies will be discouraged. In large, the me-too producer would probably loose the most. Arguing that imitative products induce pharmaceutical price competition after the patent protection or during the patent duration if clustered in Phase 3, one could suggest that without the entry of close substitutes the launching price of innovative drugs will be higher and will have a slower decreasing rate because of a lacking comparability (Lu and Comanor (1998)).

Lu and Comanor (1998) found additionally that drugs contributing important therapeutic gains were introduced at prices 3.2 times the level of substitute drugs in equivalent dosages. Drugs which achieved only modest gains were priced at 2.17 times the average for substitutes, those making little or no gain were priced approximately at the same level as substitute drugs that exist before.

Around two-thirds of all prescriptions are drugs out of the reference price limits on reimbursement clusters and which are therefore indirectly regulated (see Figure 4). The share of these drugs has not changed much since 2000, while the turnover of these drugs has dropped significantly from ca. 60% in 2000 to 35,4% in 2003. A necessary consequence of these adjustments is the reduction of turnovers, which indicates that the saving effect is mainly financed by the producers. According to VFA (2004)[19] the health insurance companies saved around 2.4 Mill. Euro in 2004.

The results for the German experiences are exactly monitored by the companies because if they are successful in the largest European Market this kind of price regulation could be adapted in other European countries as well.

[18]Skimming is a strategy of setting a high initial price and then lowering over time, penetration is a strategy of launching a new product at a low price and then rising it over time.

[19]VFA is the German Association of Research-Based Pharmaceutical Companies.

4.1.2. Patents and Parallel Imports

Economic theory considers patent protection as a second best solution to pay for R&D. The first best solution is the marginal cost pricing. With the large fixed cost of R&D the first best solution is not feasible. Marginal cost pricing provides no adequate returns to maintain a certain innovation level unless government subsidizes R&D. Therefore, patents deliver the patentees an opportunity for pricing above marginal costs and are the best attempt to finance R&D.

Given monopoly pricing then differential pricing according to the Ramsey principle, postulating prices are inversely related to demand elasticities, is consistent with the criterion of economic efficiency and general norms of equity. From this point of view price differences are not optimal if parallel imports and external reference pricing occur. A solution here could be a managed care approach where payers, normally social insurance funds or government, use their monopsony power and negotiate contracts with pharmaceutical companies that include confidential rebates and allowances. The point is that differential pricing alone can not tackle the problem of generating incentives for R&D to develop new innovative drugs and should therefore be not emphasized onesided.

But the determination of the best patent duration is still unclear. If governments try to take into account the cost to identify prices for pharmaceuticals the conclusions will be distorted in different directions. First, the complete costs of an R&D project comprise investments made over 10-15 years ago and the opportunity costs of the fixed capital. Second, the complete costs of discovering and developing a new drug also include the foregone failures or 'dry holes' (DiMasi, Hansen, and Grabowski (2003)). Third, the share of global joint cost is hard to measure. Fourth, pharmaceutical companies have no real incentives to reveal their effective costs. Rather they have in fact a reason to overestimate their R&D cost in order to have a more advantageous standpoint via government or social insurance funds while negotiating for prices of new pharmaceutical compounds. The question in dispute is whether the rate of returns in the pharmaceutical market are adequate or suboptimal, but this question can not be answered immediately because of incomplete and biased information.

Parallel trade has been argued to be consistent with principles of free trade and to lead to specific effects for patients, welfare, and the parties thereto. Firstly, as a cross-country effect the parallel trades generates in the long run uniform prices and the arbitrage will result in more efficient market operations. Secondly, a general destination country effect combined with an aggregate welfare effect will be an increased price competition that lowers the prices for pharmaceuticals which is again advantageous for patients and payers. Thirdly, patients will benefit of access to innovative new and low-priced pharmaceuticals. Fourthly, parallel imports are assumed to have only marginal effects on the pharmaceutical industry but would enhance the potential to innovate and hence improve the efficiency of this sector (Kanavos, Costa-i Font, Merkur, and Gemmill (2003)). Indeed in the short run there may be savings from lower foreign prices for patients and payers, but still the potential impact on the industry are losses of business in destination countries from the conduct of parallel trade, and decreases of producer profitability without essentially increasing social welfare. Additionally, deadweight welfare losses are possible. The authors point to the conclusion of rather low savings to health insurance institutions through direct (price) and intra- or inter-country competitive effects. Some benefits to pharmacies and marginal benefits to patients occur but parallel trade is most advantageous to parallel traders.[20]

Arguing that parallel trade is consistent with the principles of free trade then it must be noted that the fundamental condition for an efficiency gain from trade is not given, i.e. a lower foreign price does not mirror a lower social cost of production. One possible reaction to parallel imports may be to try to set rather high uniform prices for new pharmaceuticals in all countries of the European Union. This strategy will probably fail because of different national regulations.

4.2. Evaluation of Demand-Side Types

4.2.1. Drug Budget Regulation for Physicians

The aim of prescription budgets is to encourage physicians to consider cost when selecting treatments, while allowing them prescribing expensive treatments in individual cases. Examining the data of German health care market the use of drug budgets seems to be an appropriate and effective measure to induce a reflected prescribing behavior.

Figure 2.8 shows longitudinal data of prescriptions on account of sickness funds in Germany. The data is provided by the WIdO and portrays the development of total number of prescriptions to the number of prescribed drugs with undisputed effectiveness.

[20]See Figure 2.5: Savings by Reimportation in different European Countries (2002) for detailed information.

Figure 2.8: Development of prescriptions in the German Statutory Health Insurance Scheme

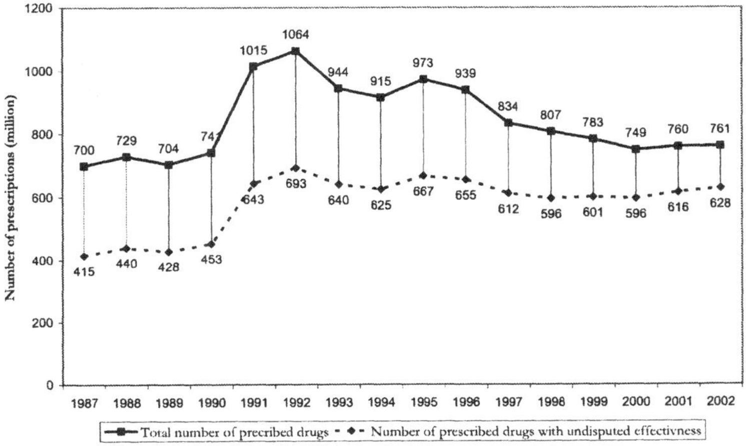

Source: Research Institute of general regional sickness funds (WIdO)

The longitudinal data disclose the change in the development of the number of prescriptions after the introduction of physicians' drug budgets in 1993. The range between the total number of prescribed and the number of drugs with undisputed effectiveness has become obvious and this reduction becomes particularly clear after the introduction of drug budgets in 1993. This is due to the increase of prescribed drugs with undisputed effectiveness, whereas the level of the total number of prescribed drugs remains more or less on the same level.

Figure 2.9 demonstrates that the change in the prescribing habit of physicians leads to a totally different expenditure pattern of the German Statutory Health Insurance scheme. Since 1992 the expenditures for prescribed drugs with disputed effectiveness has dropped by 62% and the prescription of drugs with undisputed effectiveness has risen by 69%. Considering the development of these time series it is obvious that the physicians have significantly changed their prescribing habits towards more effective prescriptions. But since the total drug costs of the Statutory Health Insurance in Germany raised it can be assumed that the savings are probably used to replace old drug therapies by innovative and more expensive ones.[21]

[21]To make more reliable statements it would be necessary to analyze the structure of the different prescribed therapies regarding their innovative level and to their respective costs.

Figure 2.9: Development of expenditures for prescribed drugs in the German Statutory Health Insurance scheme

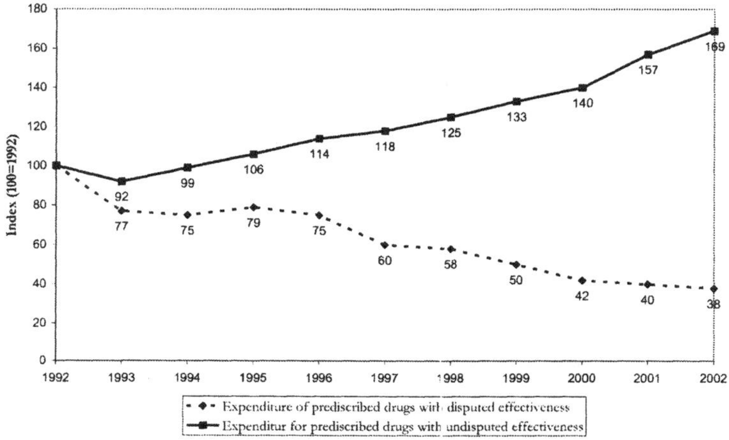

Source: Research Institute of general regional sickness funds (WIdO)

According to Schreyögg and Busse (2004) referrals to specialists particulary for treatments of chronically ill patients increased and also caused raising total drug costs years after the introduction of drug budgets. Given the prescribing restriction of physicians by the introduction of drug budgets the behavior of referral to specialists appears rational.

4.2.2. Generic Drugs

Danzon and Furukawa (2003) found that countries with strict price regulation have lower generic penetration than less regulated markets. The underlying idea is that regulation tends to reduce competition. Accordingly, in this analysis total generic share of unit volume is lower in the relatively high price-regulated markets of France (28 percent), Italy (34 percent), and Japan (40 percent), and higher in countries with less restrictive pricing policy as in the United Kingdom (49 percent), the USA (58 percent), and Germany (61 percent). The high generic share in Canada despite of high price controls is due to other regulative controls which enhance the use of generics.

In the United States the generic sector is dominated by unbranded compounds, but the total generic share of 58 percent of unit volume is confronted with only 18 percent of sales indicating relative low generic prices. In Germany the total share of 61 percent of units is confronted with 34 percent of sales, showing relatively higher generic prices. But the relative higher prices of generics in Germany are due to the reference price limits on reimbursement (Danzon and Furukawa (2003)).

The expected new form of competition after the expiration of patents varies widely from country to country caused by legal obstacles, incomplete information, reimbursement regulations hence the price elasticity of patients, pharmacy dispensing margins and different preferences of the prescribing physicians for the original brand versus generic drugs. As the case may be, the lower the price of generic drugs the higher the health care cost savings will be. Considering these many influencing factors the incentives to subsidy original brand drugs by generic drugs have to be well-thought out. Reference pricing as applied in Germany is expected to increase the prescription of generic drugs because reference prices are usually based on rather low priced products in each class without regarding the actual patent situation. Alternatively, if the pharmacy dispensing margins are more favorably and the drug budgets for physician are fixed, the probability of generic prescription will also increase. In general, complete unregulated pricing is not given but rather a range of price regulations are applied and therefore the different interactions have to be taken into account with regard to the desired outcome.

5. Implications and Conclusions

In the past most regulative measures to contain health care expenditures have been targeted primarily to supply-side measures, however this is changing into a more sophisticated regulative construct. But, supply-side regulation on its own does little to control the rising expenditures. Without simultaneous use of demand-side incentives and volume controls, pharmaceutical expenditures probably can not be reduced effectively.

What makes the German pharmaceutical price regulation effective is the combination of demand side regulation with physicians' drug budgets, proportional co-payments with upper and lower caps, and the usage of reference price limits on reimbursement. Opponents of current national pharmaceutical price regulation argue that one principle problem occurring in systems of controlling health care expenditures is that much of the pharmaceutical expenditures are spend regardless of the quality of the medicine or treatment reduction.

The standard argument that the R&D location is in the country where the highest profits can be made is not correct. It can be observed that national firms do not research in the country with the highest turnovers, rather they research where the research circumstances, in terms of innovative regional clusters, are the best. Proponents of standard international trade theory often support parallel trading as a way for enhancing competition and in consequence reducing drug prices. But usually standard trade theory is led by the assumption that prices reflect efficiency in production or high or rather low input prices. Considering the drug prices, the situation appears more difficult. Low drug prices in several countries reflect severe governmental price regulations (Danzon (1997b)).

As a matter of principle, national governments have to decide what sociopolitical goals to follow. Designing different scenarios the point of departure could be intergenerational fairness, meaning that the present generation leaves its successors sufficient wealth so that persons deciding behind a veil of ignorance would be indifferent as to whether they want to be born today or tomorrow.

Chapter 3

Health Care Expenditures, Ageing Population and Pharmaceutical Innovation

1. Introduction

Why should an ageing population be a problem? Some argue that an ageing population inherently causes high future health care expenditures (HCE), therefore controlling health care expenditures appears reasonable. Several studies forecasting health care spending predict continuously increasing expenses due to at least three different factors; ageing, technical progress, and increasing prices. Here we look in particular at pharmaceutical innovations and expenditures on pharmaceuticals. Whether the effects of pharmaceutical innovations are cost driving or cost lowering with respect to expenditures on prescribed drugs (EPD) will be analyzed and evaluated with regard to their current impact. Arguing as for total health expenditures that the corresponding proximity to death is integrant and not the age per se then this proximity would be the crucial element for rising expenses. Though in older age cohorts there are more people in their last life span. Therefore in cohorts of 65 aged and over it is important to determine whether more and more pharmaceuticals are prescribed as a vain attempt to avert death which in consequence causes disproportionate high pharmaceutical expenditures, or whether the expectancy of life is increasing by medical progress or by a more healthy way of living. Then an increasing share of people of 65 years and over (we call henceforth the share of 65+) can be an extenuating factor on pharmaceutical expenditures because the idiosyncratic mortality rates will decrease, and in each age cohort there would be less persons in their last life span. Then the increase of the share of 65+ should lead to decreasing age specific EPD over time. The attempt to sketch the situation indicates that there must be a kind of multiplicative or rather interdependent relationship between influencing factors such as pharmaceutical expenditures, medical progress, and age structure.

In fact, the expenditures on pharmaceuticals are one of the crucial factors of HCE. But they have hardly ever been analyzed regarding influences as demographic change or the effects of pharmaceutical innovation. As the pharmaceutical market is also an interesting one this growth market should therefore not be neglected considering there influences due to pharmaceutical innovations as more and more governments try to contain rising EPD and hence rising HCE. Also the international quantitative analysis on macro data appears to be somewhat unusual. To close these gaps an international dynamic panel data analysis including most relevant countries will be applied.

The paper is structured as follows. Section 2 examines the theoretical framework of the way in which demographic change and pharmaceutical innovation may affect the HCE and expenditures on pharmaceuticals. Section 3 presents the data and specified models. Section 4 describes the employed methodology. Section 5 discusses the empirical results. Finally, in section 6 conclusion will be drawn.

2. Theoretical Review of the Determinants of HCE

Demographical change and medical progress can be seen as reciprocate boosting or extenuating factors on health care expenditures (Breyer (2000)). Demographical change and medical progress defined as interactive factors can result in different outcomes. For instance, HCE boosting factors can be described in the interdependent relationship defined as the Sisyphus Syndrome in health care or multimorbidity hypothesis. The first functional chain is developed by Zweifel and Ferrari (1992). They argue that if modern medicine is effective in increasing changes of survival by lowering resources in other economic sectors in order to increase the resource allocation in the health care sector then this must result in increased longevity. If so

the increased number of aging survivors will ask for more medical services. To spin the thought out the more resources allocated to health care services the greater the achievements of medical progress in terms of longevity. And again the longer the life span the higher the HCE.[1]
Alternatively, rising HCE could be founded on the multimorbidity of older patients. Without medical progress the initially heterogeneous population will develop due to selective mortality to a rather homogenous population of old-aged persons that have been proven to be the fittest. If the mortality rate decreases as a result of medical progress than the selection is slowed down and there are left more sick old-aged persons. The successful medical combat of one disease, for instance cardiovascular disease, would increase longevity without making them healthier but inducing the next disease to be medicated e.g. cancer (Krämer (1996)). The multimorbidity hypothesis is based upon the experience that the human body in toto has a certain expected lifetime. Transgressing this will lead to a successive collapse of organs. This second functional chain is reasoned on the assumption that the patients do get older by medical progress but do not get healthier. Therefore, medical progress only increases longevity of sick patients who will die anyway. The increase of the hazard rate to survive is connected to the reduction of an average state of health in population. If the multimorbidity thesis proves to be true then it maybe economically rational to reduce treatments or pharmaceuticals because they would only be a vain attempt to avert death which would lead to disproportionate high pharmaceutical and/or health care expenditures without increasing the expectancy of life. Accordingly, Krämer (1996) argues that the extension of life time is mainly spent in sick bed.
These two functional chains imply that HCE can not be simply added to the regression analyzes because there is a moderation effect by medical progress and political demand for medical services onto the number of patients that will be treated (Breyer (2000)).[2]
Demographical change and medical progress seen as extenuating factors on health care expenditures is founded on other aspects. Fuchs' (1984) most important findings show that in fact there is a very large increase in life expectancy at aged 65 and a very large increase since 1976

[1]The empirical evidences of the Sisyphus Syndrome using OECD data shown by Zweifel and Ferrari (1992) argue for an expenditure effect in form of a prolongation of the remaining life expectancy (RLE) at ages 40 and 65. The revisited analysis of the Sisyphus Syndrome by Zweifel, Steinmann, and Eugster (2005) could identify signs of politically and economically positive feedback effects caused ageing population, although the Sisyphus Syndrome cycle seemed to have abated lately.

[2]Several studies proved the multimorbidity hypothesis to be wrong, for instance Dinkel (1999).

in real per capita health care expenditures on the elderly relative to expenditure on person under age 65. But a cross-sectional analysis showed that the increase with age in per capita health care expenditure is primarily attributable to very large expenditure in the last year of life. Consequently, the determined differences of HCE between younger and older patients can not be purely ascribed to the age but according to the cross-sectional analysis to the different proximities to death. Taken this in regard then in older age cohorts there are assumable more people in their last life span. If caused by medical progress and a more healthy way of living, the mortality rate will decrease in each cohort and there will be fewer people in their last life span.[3] Thus medical progress connected to more healthy way of living can lead to a reduction of proximity to death interval and therefore to a decline of age related HCE in the corresponding cohorts. The over-all effect due to the medical progress could be the decrease of HCE for an ageing population.[4]

3. Determinants of Pharmaceutical Expenditures

3.1. Data and Descriptive Statistics

As expenditures on prescribed drugs (EPD) have grown faster than any other major components of HCE since the late 1990s, cross-national differences in pharmaceutical expenditures are of great interest (DiMasi, Hansen, and Grabowski (2003)). In the following panel analysis we will investigate the effects caused by ageing and pharmaceutical progress on EPD. We will use data of seven countries namely Australia, Canada, Finland, France, Germany, Japan and USA over a period of 11 years from 1991 to 2001 in order to analyze these effects. An advantage of using international comparison or rather macroeconomic evaluation methods is to ask positive questions such as: Does ageing and pharmaceutical industry activity concerning R&D have any effect on the EPD or pharmaceutical innovations; do increasing doctors' consultations lead to rising EPD; or does an ageing population cause an increase of R&D activity?

[3]This kind of development is also known as the compression of mortality or rather the compression hypothesis. According to Fries (1985) the increasing rectangular survival curve, with obvious convergence of curves from different decades, portrays visually the limits of human life span.

[4]There are many evidences that the medical costs are considerably rising with increasing proximity to death, for instance Lubitz, Beebe, and Baker (1995) or Zweifel, Felder, and Meier (1996).

Before starting with the descriptive statistics the data construction should be mentioned. We use the OECD Health Data (2005) including the total health care expenditures (HCE), expenditures on prescribed drugs (EPD) and over-the counter drugs (EOD), as well as the R&D expenditures of the pharmaceutical industry and the GDP all given in per capita in US$ purchasing power parities (PPP).[5] Additionally, we use the data from the same source including the health status such as further life expectancy at age 65 (LIFEXP65) or the population age structure including the share of people of 65 age and over (POP65). The health care utilization we captured by incorporating the doctors' consultation in number per capita. From the annual report of the European Patent Office the patent applications has been used as a proxy for the pharmaceutical innovations.

Figure 3.1: Development of health care expenditures and expenditures on prescribed drugs in Australia, Canada, Finland, and France*, 1991-2001

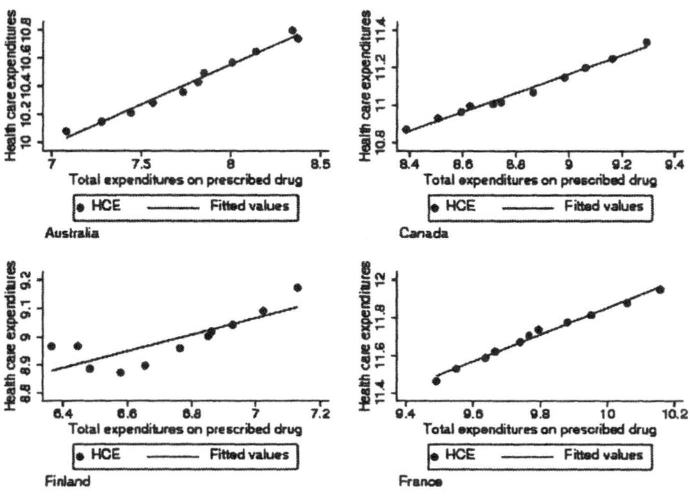

Source: own estimations

* Health care expenditures and expenditures on prescribed drugs are given as PPP, Million US$.

[5]The PPP are used because the rates of currency conversion equalize the purchasing power of different currencies across full range of goods and services contained in pharmaceutical goods. Therefore the differences in price levels between countries are eliminated.

After gaining an overview of the data that have been used we should take a look at the descriptive statistics. As can be seen in Figures 3.1 and 3.2 illustrating the development of HCE and EPD there is a monotonous rising trend for almost all countries. In Australia HCE and EPD increased until 2000 and decreased slightly in 2001. Canada faced rising HCE and EPD for the complete considered period of 11 years. In Finland 1991 and 1992 HCE stagnated and EPD rose but 1993 HCE dropped whereas EPD was continuously rising. In the years after 1994 EPD and HCE continued to increase. During the same time France faced no reduction of HCE and EPD during the whole considered period.

Germany was successful in reducing the EPD and experienced a decline in the period between of 1991 to 1993. But after 1993 HCE and EPD rose continuously to the end of the observation period. In Japan we observe increasing HCE and for EPD a kind of two years steps rising in 1991 to 1992 and 1993 to 1994. In 1996 to 1998 EPD decreased while HCE still increased. 1998 Japan also faced rising HCE and EPD until 2001. The US HCE had a steeper gradient in comparison to the EPD until 1997 but since 1997 to 2001 EPD rose faster than HCE did.

Figure 3.2: Development of health care expenditures and expenditures on prescribed drugs in Germany, Japan, and USA*, 1991-2001

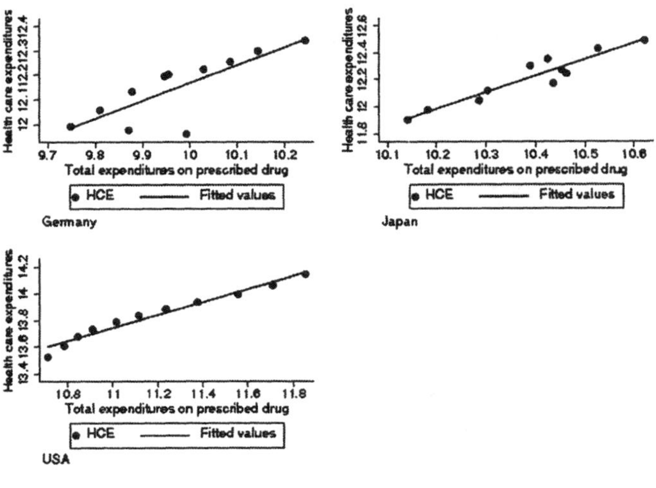

Source: own estimations

* Health care expenditures and expenditures on prescribed drugs are given as PPP, Million US$.

3.2. The Models

Based upon these previous considerations we assume several functional chains which have been specified in different hypotheses. These different hypotheses include total health care expenditures, total expenditures on prescribed (EPD) and over-the-counter drugs (EOD) as well as innovations measured as patent applications. In order to consider supply and demand components we take into account different regressors. We expect that the share of 65+ will act as a demand component or rather pull factor of EPD and innovations. We subsume the R&D expenditures of pharmaceutical industry and health care utilization measured as doctors' consultations will cover the supply components or rather push factors of EPD and innovations. According to our a priori hypotheses we assume that increasing push and pull factors will cause rising EPD and innovations. For instance, an increase of the share of 65+ will lead to increasing EPD. Or rising R&D activity of pharmaceutical industry will cause a supply induced increase of EPD but not for EOD. As intensified R&D activity of pharmaceutical industry will cause an increase of innovative drugs that will be patented and therefore necessarily be prescribed, EOD should not be affected by this kind of innovative activity.

To sum up, we conjecture a positive relationship between the different regressors and the expenditures on prescribed drugs. Accordingly, we formulate four hypotheses, three of which concerning the age-specific interactions and one concerning pharmaceutical innovations. The first three age specific hypotheses are as follows:

1. Hypothesis:

If the share of 65+ (pull factor) as well as the doctors' consultations (push factor) increase, total health care expenditures will increase. But if R&D expenditures of pharmaceutical industry (push factor) increase then HCE will decrease because a substitution effect between innovative drugs and more expensive medical technology such as a surgery.

2. Hypothesis:

If the share of 65+ as well as the doctors' consultations and R&D expenditures of pharmaceutical industry increase, the total expenditures on prescribed drugs will increase.

3. Hypothesis:

The share of 65+ as well as the doctors' consultations and R&D expenditures of pharmaceutical industry are not expected to determine total expenditures on over the counter drugs.

Behind this hypothesis lies the assumption that pharmaceutical industry is particularly interested in innovative medicines for dominating health problems of elderly which are mostly chronic diseases, in particular cardiovascular, metabolic, muscle and skeleton disease, malignant growth, and psychological diseases for instance dementia and depressions.

We can imagine different procedures to measure innovations on pharmaceuticals, for instance taking into account patents or pharmaceutical R&D spending. According to Scherer (2001) the relationship between profitability and R&D expenditures can be described in three ways. First, successful R&D leads with a long lag to new products which depending on the market penetration can add greatly to the business profits. Second, realized profits can act as a source of funds to support R&D expenditures. And finally, managers' expectations of future profit opportunities which are anchored by contemporary market conditions can induce a demand-pull influence on R&D expenditures. Barzel (1968) showed that innovations are induced, since they become more profitable with the expansion of output. But the resulting amount of resources dedicated to innovating activity would not be optimal. The inability of innovators to acquire all benefits may tend to make the amount too small. But if the innovations are launched at their optimal dates then their contribution to wealth will be greater than it could have been by the same resources employed elsewhere in the economy. As the competition between potential innovators may deprive innovations of all their special economic value, the author concludes that the increasing number of innovations tends to make the R&D spending too large.

In our panel data we do not have data about profits, so we try to circumvent this by using other proxies. Namely, we regard patent applications as instruments for pharmaceutical innovation. The considered patent applications are categorized according to the International Patent Classification (IPC) indices.[6] These include inter alia A61K[7], A61M[8], and A61F[9].

[6]The interrelation between profits and innovation is ambiguous. It is not clear whether the causality runs from profit to innovation or from innovation to profits or whether there is no causal relationship (U.S. General Accounting Office (GAO) (1994)).

[7]A61K is including preparations for medical, dental, or toilet purposes.

[8]A61M is including devices for introducing media into, or onto, the body.

[9]A61F is including filters implantable into blood vessels; prostheses; devices providing patency to, or preventing collapsing of, tubular structures of the body, for instance stents; orthopaedic, nursing or contraceptive devices; fomentation; treatment or protection of eyes or ears; bandages; dressing or absorbent pads; first-aid kits.

Figure 3.3: Medical patent applications in the 30 European Patent Convention (EPC) member states, 1990-2004

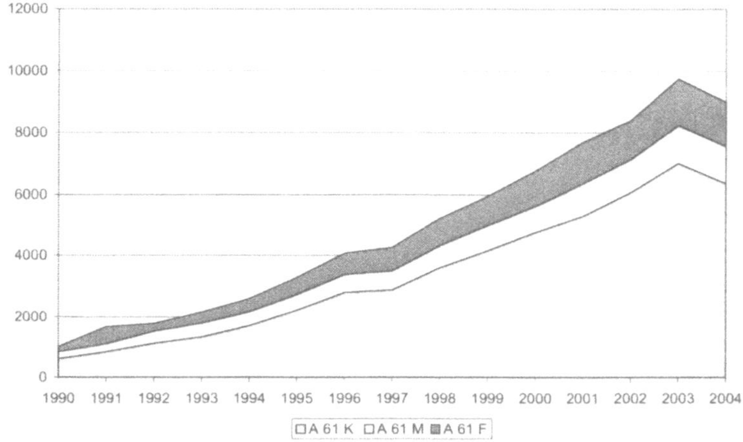

Source: WIPO (2005)

As Figure 3.3 shows, the largest share of patent applications are A61K including preparation for medical purposes. Keeping in mind the mentioned arguments, the hypotheses for pharmaceutical innovations are defined as follows:

4.1. Hypothesis:

If the further life expectancy at age 65 (pull factor) as well as the R&D expenditures of the pharmaceutical industry (push factor) increase, the innovations instrumented as patent applications will increase.

The extension of this hypothesis includes an additional exogenous regressor, namely the specific national GDP. The supposition behind this extension is that the current national GDP is assumed to act as a push factor. If the economy is growing it is assumed that the number of innovations proxied by as patent applications will also increase. This thought leads to the last hypothesis which is defined as follows:

4.2. Hypothesis:

If the further life expectancy at age 65 (pull factor) as well as the R&D expenditures of the pharmaceutical industry increase, and the current national GDP (push factors) increase, innovations instrumented as patent applications will increase.

In the last two hypotheses it is assumed that an increase in the further life expectancy will enhance the pharmaceutical innovations because rising life expectancy will enforce the need for medicines dedicated to the elderly due to increasing multimorbidity. Keeping in mind these hypotheses in the following chapter, we will continue with the methodology.

4. Methodology

4.1. Overview

Over the last thirty years statistical models which are combining cross sectional and time series data have become more and more common. Important advantages of such panel data are the number of observations are usually higher and more detailed, the double dimension, and problems like multicollinearity are reduced, because the independent variables differ in two dimensions and are therefore less probable to be highly correlated. As mentioned above in the following estimation part panel data the OECD Health Data (2005) will be used. It is a longitudinal survey, in which a given set of countries are repeatedly sampled at different points of time. In this survey the several observations are available for almost every country. As some argue that cross-sectional data mirror short-term effects and time series data capture the long-run effects. The combination of these two types of data leads to the crucial characteristics of panel data with which one is able to formulate and estimate dynamic structures (Balestra (1995)).
The crucial step in estimating is to decide in which way the reality can be modeled in the most appropriated way. According to the different sets of underlying assumptions the chosen model will vary. Thus a principal step is to design heterogenous behaviour. Heterogeneity may turn up in regression coefficients because they differ across countries and/or in time, or in the structure of the residuals. With the intention to keep the model simple only country specific differences are looked at for the moment.
Unfortunately, the one and only universally valid specification does not exist. Depending on the type of problem and the characteristics of the data one has to choose an useful specification (Balestra (1995)). Two alternative specifications, the within estimator and the first-differenced generalized method of moments (GMM) estimator will be applied. The GMM estimator is a dynamic panel estimator. The motivation for this is that there are observations for a number of

countries, with various observations for each country, and that the lagged values of the dependent variable are assumed to affect the actual dependent variable.[10]

4.2. Estimation Specification

Considering an autoregressive panel data model of the general form:

$$y_{it} = \delta y_{it-1} + \beta' x_{it} + u_{it} \tag{3.1}$$

and

$$u_{it} = \mu_i + \varepsilon_{it} \tag{3.2}$$

with $i = 1, ..., N$ as an index for the different countries and $t = 1, ..., T$ as a time index and $|\delta| < 1$. Corresponding to the usual one way error component model, equation (2) contains the error u_{it}, which is composed of a time-invariant country specific effect μ_i and a random noise ε_{it}. A one way error component model implies that the time specific effects have uniform consequences upon all variables.

Probably the easiest and most plausible way to take into account the country specific and/or time differences connected with panel data regression problems is to stipulate that some of the regression coefficients are permitted to vary across countries and/or with time. Assume the regression coefficients are not known, but fixed. As noted in equation (2), the error term in this model is assumed to include a time-invariant country specific effect μ_i and also a random noise ε_{it}, which means the intercept is permitted to vary from country to country, but the slope parameter are assumed to be constant in both country and time proportions (Ahn and Schmidt (1995)). This one way error component structure has country specific and time invariant effects (μ_i) without time variant effects (λ_t) because only short periods are considered and the underlying assumption is that time effects affect all countries in the same way. Therefore the country invariant and time variant effect is zero ($\lambda_t = 0$).[11]

[10]Note that, when a dynamic panel data model includes a lagged dependent explanatory variable and as a result the usually employed estimation procedures are asymptotically valid only when the number of observations in the time dimension (T) gets large (Kiviet (1995)).

[11]An alternative assumption would be a two way error component model which is defined as $u_{it} = \mu_i + \lambda_t + \varepsilon_{it}$ and only put $\lambda_t = 0$, but with regard to point of departure it is logical to imply an one way error component model.

The fixed-effect approach[12] is chosen, because the pre-analysis provided results which rejected the random effect approach[13] according to the Hausman specification test. An advantage of using the within estimator is that to estimate the coefficients the individual effects are not necessary. By using the least squares after transforming into deviations from means, the individual effects are eliminated from equation (1) and we only consider intra-country variations or the variation within groups. The problem is that the within estimator is inconsistent because the within transformation causes a correlation of order $\frac{1}{T}$ between the lagged dependent variable and the residuum. Although the within estimator has an approximation error, in simulations studies Kiviet (1995) found that it was astonishingly accurate.

In order to avoid this problem another specification is used, the first-differenced Generalized Method of Moment (GMM) estimator proposed by Arellano and Bond (1991). Due to heteroscedasticity we did not use instrumental variables (IV) estimation. In this case the GMM estimator is more efficient than the IV estimator.

The general form of the GMM estimator including the different underlying assumptions will be stated. It is assumed that μ_i and ε_{it} have the well-known error component structure:

$$E(\mu_i) = 0, \quad E(\varepsilon_{it}) = 0, \quad E(\varepsilon_{it}\mu_i) = 0 \quad for \quad i = 1, ...N \quad and \quad t = 2, ..., T \tag{3.3}$$

and

$$E(\varepsilon_{it}\varepsilon_{is}) = 0 \quad for \quad i = 1, ...N \quad and \quad \forall \quad t \neq s. \tag{3.4}$$

The next assumption affects the initial condition, as proposed by Ahn and Schmidt (1995), among others

$$E(y_{i1}\varepsilon_{it}) = 0 \quad for \quad i = 1, ...N \quad and \quad t = 2, ..., T. \tag{3.5}$$

Equation (2), (3), and (4) describe the standard assumptions that indicate moment restrictions which are satisfactory to estimate and also identify δ for $T \geq 3$.

In cases like ours it is important to acquire consistent although maybe less efficient estimators of certain parameters. This can be achieved by using method of moments. To shun the problem that the dependent lagged variable is correlated with the error term, we consider the Generalized Method of Moment (GMM). The suggested solution for this problem is to first differentiate the equation with the purpose to get rid of the time invariant individual effects and later estimate

[12]The fixed-effect approach uses the within regression estimator.

[13]The random effect approaches uses the between regression estimator.

the model with instrumental variables (IV). The IV in this specification are dependent variables lagged with two periods. The explanation is obvious, because in the dynamic model the dependent variable enters into the equations as one period lagged and the IV is nothing else than the one period lagged dependent variable lagged with another period. Therefore, the IV is the dependent variable lagged with two periods. The result that is hoped for is to achieve a consistent, although inefficient estimator, because this estimator does not use all existing moment conditions (Ahn and Schmidt (1995)).

In order to obtain the first-difference of the equation this proceeding takes away permanent unobserved heterogeneity caused by the different countries. Additionally, Arellano and Bond (1991) emphasize that the crucial identification condition for estimating a dynamic model from panel data is the strict exogeneity of some of the explanatory variables[14] conditional on the unobservable individual effects (Arellano and Bond (1991)).

The first-differenced GMM estimator is obviously constructed upon first differences, which removes the individual that means country specific effects.[15] Therefore, we generally note for all hypotheses:

$$\Delta y_{it} = \delta' \Delta y_{it-1} + \gamma' \Delta \phi_{it} + \gamma' \Delta \phi_{it-1} + \sum_{k=1}^{K} \beta_k' \Delta x_{it}^k + \Delta u_{it}. \tag{3.6}$$

The error component structure can be similarly described by equation (2), (3), and (4). If we do not allow any further assumptions as the basis for the process that generates the standard assumptions, in other words the initial conditions, together with our autoregressive error components we suggest the following $m_d = \frac{1}{2}(T-1)(T-2)$ orthogonality conditions that are linear in the δ parameter. We generally note,

$$E(y_{it-s} \Delta u_{it}) = 0 \quad with \quad t = 3, ..., T \quad and \quad 2 \leq s \leq t-1. \tag{3.7}$$

We can assume these additional restrictions, because in (4) we supposed that there is no serial correlation in the time variant disturbance ε_{it}. Together with the standard assumption noted in (5), the moment conditions that are implied in equation (7) are plausible (Ahn and Schmidt (1995)).

Using lagged values of the dependent variables is an attempt to avoid problems of interdependence between the dependent and predetermined variables. We follow the supposition that the

[14] Or alternative, just the availability of strictly exogenous IV.

[15] $\Delta u_{it} = u_{it} - u_{it-1} = \mu_i + \varepsilon_{it} - (\mu_i + \varepsilon_{it-1}) = \varepsilon_{it} - \varepsilon_{it-1}$

lagged values will reduce these interdependence problems.[16] It is advisable to assume that the dependent variables and the predetermined variables are acquired simultaneously. Continuing this line of thought and assuming that R&D expenditures of pharmaceutical industry are predetermined in the fourth hypothesis concerning innovation there are only $\frac{1}{2}(T-1)(T-2)$ additional moment condition and we write $E(\Phi_{is}\varepsilon_{it}) \neq o$ for $s \leq t$. As a result of this assumption and in combination with the assumptions (4) and (5) we can construct the linear moment condition (Hujer, Blien, Caliendo, and Zeiss (2002)). We write:

$$E(\Phi_{it-s}\Delta u_{it}) = 0, \quad for \quad t = 3,...,T \quad and \quad 2 \leq s \leq t-1. \tag{3.8}$$

In the set of explanatory variables, including doctors' consultations, further life expectancy for 65 aged and over, the share of 65+, which are strictly exogenous, the additional T(T-2) moment conditions are valid and we assume $E(X_{it}\varepsilon_{it}) = 0 \ \forall \ s, t$. Following the circumstance that the x_{it} process is strictly exogenous, the additional moment condition:

$$E(x_{is}\Delta u_{it}) = 0, \quad t = 3,...,T \quad and \quad 1 \leq s \leq T \tag{3.9}$$

is valid (Blundell, Bond, and Windmeijer (2000)). By using this proposal of Arellano and Bond (1991) we are able to compute the one-step estimators β_1^y in one step. If the disturbances ε_{it} in the specifications are i.i.d., the one-step and the two-step estimates of the first-differenced GMM estimator is equal in the specific models (Blundell and Bond (1998)).

However, before starting with the estimation we should keep in mind that the GMM estimator is consistent only if the number of countries becomes very large, but in our sample we have only data from seven countries. Therefore, it is possible that problems during the estimation process can arise. And on the basis of this rather small sample we have to keep in mind problems like multicollinearity.

Note that, although the within estimator are used to estimate the implemented hypotheses, the dynamic relation of the expenditures on prescribed drugs or the innovations cannot be captured. In addition, our dynamic panel data model suffers from simultaneity and identification problems like all macroeconomic studies which can be solved by theoretical foundation. This fiddly 'chicken-or-egg' query has obviously no simple solution. We tried to solve the key identification problem this case by using variables that are highly correlated with explanatory variables without being part of the dependent variable equation.

[16] See equation (6).

Summing up, these two alternative specifications (the basic equations for the dynamic panel estimator and the within estimator) will be applied for the HCE, the EPD, the EOD equations on one side, and on the other side the pharmaceutical innovations equations.

5. Results

We turn now to the results of the different estimators. Using the natural logarithm values of the dependent and independent variables a log-linear model results which has the attractive feature that the slope coefficients measure the elasticity of the explanatory variable with respect to the explaining variables.
As shown in Table 3.1 the within groups estimation results[17] provide highly significant coefficients in the HCE equation for POP65 and R&D expenditures. The positive signs indicate that an increase of the pull and push factors will induce a rising of HCE. In our hypothesis we assumed that rising R&D activity will cause decreasing HCE but this is not mirrored in the within groups estimation. Concerning the EPD we found significant results for all regressors although we expected EPD to increase with more frequent doctors' consultations. In accordance with our assumptions we found no effects for the EOD besides highly significant positive effects for R&D expenditures. The hypothesis 4.1 is confirmed in the within groups estimation. The alternative hypothesis 4.2 is almost confirmed but the R&D expenditures do not become significant any longer since GDP is additionally considered. The fixed effect specification appears to be justified since no hypotheses confirmed that the country specific error term is equal to zero.
Table 3.2 depicts the first-differenced GMM estimation results. We found the first hypothesis confirmed with at least marginally significant effects for all variables. The one period lagged endogenous regressors are significant in all hypotheses. HCE is highly significant in both lagged periods. But there is a change of sign in the second lag of HCE. This can be explained by the endeavour of countries to contain HCE. Viewing the moving average growth rates of HCE in fact this kind of development can be observed. After several years of rising HCE each of the considered countries faced a reduction of the moving average growth rates in the

[17] Blundell, Bond, and Windmeijer (2000) argue that the within groups estimators are biased downwards as well as the first-differenced GMM estimators.

following years and then again HCE continued to increase. For instance, 1991 and 1992 the moving average growth rates for HCE in Finland first decreased and then increased again for the following three years and then decreased. There is also a change of sign for EPD and again it can be assumed that governments search for possibilities to contain EPD which can be retrieved in the data including the moving average growth rates of EPD.

Table 3.1: Fixed effects estimation results

Hypothesis:	(1)	(2)	(3)	(4.1)	(4.2)
Regressand:	HCE	DRUG	OTC	PATENT	PATENT
Regressors:					
CONSTANT	5.988^a	4.121^a	5.850^a	-30.769^a	-40.112^a
(std. err.)	(0.542)	(0.952)	(0.753)	(3.564)	(3.494)
POP65	1.511^a	0.860^b	0.803		
(std. err.)	(0.239)	(0.420)	(0.332)		
LIFEXP65				11.151^a	8.358^a
(std. err.)				(1.390)	(1.289)
DOC	-0.120	-0.838^b	-0.324		
(std. err.)	(0.191)	(0.335)	(0.265)		
PHARM_R&D	0.238^a	0.660^a	0.355^a	0.792^a	0.240
(std. err.)	(0.046)	(0.952)	(0.000)	(0.121)	(0.146)
GDP					1.544^a
(std. err.)					(0.292)
σ_μ	0.813	0.757	1.070	1.160	1.835
σ_ε	0.122	0.140	0.111	0.195	0.165
F test	66.73	52.99	18.96	218.29	212.70
(p-value)	(0.0000)	(0.0000)	(0.0000)	(0.0000)	(0.0000)
R^2_{within}	0.7665	0.7227	0.7337	0.8652	0.9050
$F(\mu_i = 0)$	250.08	37.72	150.61	90.81	124.63
(p-value)	(0.0000)	(0.0000)	(0.0000)	(0.0000)	(0.0000)

$^{a,\ b,\ c}$ Significance at 1%, 5%, 10% (All values are given in natural logarithm).

Note:

(i) HCE = Health Care Expenditures, DRUG = Expenditures on prescribed drugs, OTC = Expenditures on OTC drugs, DOC = doctors' consultations in number per capita, POP65 = Population age structure of 65 aged and older, PHARM_R&D = Expenditures of pharmaceutical industry for R&D, and PATENT = Patent application inter alia for IPC indices A61K, A61M, and A61F.

Table 3.2: First-differenced GMM estimation results

Hypothesis	(1)	(2)	(3)	(4.1)	(4.2)
Regressand:	HCE	DRUG	OTC	PATENT	PATENT
Endogen regressors:					
HCE_{t-1}	1.024[a]				
(std. err.)	(0.147)				
HCE_{t-2}	-0.408[a]				
(std. err.)	(0.112)				
$DRUG_{t-1}$		0.646[a]			
(std. err.)		(0.207)			
$DRUG_{t-2}$		-0.017			
(std. err.)		(0.150)			
OTC_{t-1}			0.812[a]		
(std. err.)			(0.191)		
OTC_{t-2}			0.103		
(std. err.)			(0.168)		
$PATENT_{t-1}$				0.451[a]	0.421[b]
(std. err.)				(0.098)	(0.098)
$PATENT_{t-2}$				0.297[a]	0.250[b]
(std. err.)				(0.096)	(0.099)
Predetermined variable:					
$\Delta PHARM\_R\&D_t$	-0.002[b]	0.005[c]	-0.005	0.166[c]	0.259[b]
(std. err.)	(0.001)	(0.003)	(0.004)	(0.091)	(0.104)
$PHARM\_R\&D_{t-1}$				-0.293[b]	-0.315[a]
(std. err.)				(0.116)	(0.116)
Exogenous regressors:					
$\Delta POP65_t$	0.005[b]	0.018[b]	0.005		
(std. err.)	(0.002)	(0.007)	(0.007)		
$\Delta LIFEXP65_t$				0.018[a]	-0.007
(std. err.)				(0.005)	(0.014)
ΔDOC_t	0.010[c]	-0.024[b]	0.011		
(std. err.)	(0.005)	(0.014)	(0.014)		
ΔGDP_t					0.006[c]
(std. err.)					(0.003)
Wald test of joint significance	11.37	7.09	0.62	14.24	10.19
(Prob > F)	(0.0000)	(0.0005)	(0.6070)	(0.0004)	(0.0002)
Arellano-Bond test autocov. in residuals of order 1 = 0	-1.50	-2.26	-4.00	-2.67	-2.88
(Prob > z)	(0.1331)	(0.0240)	(0.0001)	(0.0075)	(0.0040)
Arellano-Bond test autocov. in residuals of order 2 = 0	0.09	0.58	-0.70	0.02	0.14
(Prob > z)	(0.9293)	(0.5616)	(0.4858)	(0.9844)	(0.8897)
Hansen-Sargan test	36.50	22.09	26.71	67.34	64.47
(Prob > chi^2)	(0.0192)	(0.3941)	(0.1807)	(0.0514)	(0.0819)

[a, b, c] Significance at 1%, 5%, 10%. (All values are given in natural logarithm.)

The second hypothesis is almost confirmed but the sign of doctors' consultations is still negative. Increasing doctors' consultations lead to increasing HCE which can be due to following up therapies. Whereas increasing doctors' consultations lead to decreasing EPD. This can be caused by successful application of lower medical therapies or also by additional following up non-medical therapies which are not affecting EPD. Rising R&D activity (push factor) and the share of 65+ (pull factor) lead to increasing EPD. Although the GMM estimation provides significant coefficients, the sizes are quite moderate due to the downward biases of this estimator. The third hypothesis is fully confirmed: there are no significant effects for the considered regressors. Hypothesis 4.1 is completely confirmed except for the lagged variable R&D activity in $t-1$. In accordance with our hypothesis increasing pharmaceutical industry activity in the current period t as well as the further life expectancy at age 65 and older lead to increasing innovations measured as patent applications. The unexpected change of sign may be due to the fact that the patent application data include other IPC indices than A61K, A61M and A61F. Examining the data for the R&D expenditures none of the countries faced continuous rising growth rates for R&D expenditures which can be due to the different political and economical developments in the considered countries. Nevertheless, R&D expenditures of the pharmaceutical industry have relative strong effect onto the size of patent applications. With including GDP in the innovation hypothesis 4.2 we found significant effects for GDP and R&D activity of pharmaceutical industry but the further life expectancy becomes insignificant.

In order to test the different specifications, a Wald test of joint significance and a test for first- and second-order serial correlation is reported.[18] The Wald test statistics only rejected the null hypothesis $\beta = 0$ for the third hypothesis in the first-differenced GMM estimation concerning expenditures on OTC drugs. This is not surprising since the included regressors should determine influencing factors for HCE and EPD. The test for first-order serial correlation can not reject the null, i.e. there is evidence for serial correlated errors for all hypothesis in the GMM specification except the first hypothesis. No second-order correlation at all can be detected in GMM specification. The Hansen-Sargan test of overidentifying restrictions can not reject the set of instruments in the second and third hypothesis but in the first and the fourth hypothesis. The joint null hypothesis in this test is that the excluded instruments are valid instruments, i.e., uncorrelated with the error term. A rejection as for hypothesis 1 and 4.1 casts doubt on the

[18]See Greene (2003) for the Wald test of joint significance and Arellano and Bond (1991) for the test on serial correlation.

validity of the instruments. But now let us continue with the conclusion and implication of the results which leads us to the next section.

6. Implications and Conclusions

As EPD become a progressively larger proportion of HCE, economic evaluations are being used to inform government decision-makers and health-care organizations to supplement clinical evidence of safety and efficacy, for policy developments, for reimbursement negotiations, for resource management, and occasionally for regulation and price control. With the international expansion of markets for pharmaceuticals and the globalization of the drug industry, multinational economic evaluations could play an important role in public policy and corporate decisions. Nevertheless, few multinational economic evaluations have been published and the analytic methods for cross-national comparison are relatively underdeveloped. The lack of uniformity in data and pricing complicates multinational comparison. More macroeconomic theorization about health expenditures is necessary (Gerdtham and Jönsson (2000)).
What we found on a macroeconomic level is that HCE seems to be affected by the rising share of the 65+. However this can be explained with proximity to death but this question can not be analyzed within our data. There is evidence supported by all specifications that expenditures on prescribed drugs are affected by demographical change (pull factor) as well as by R&D expenditures (push factor). These results indicate that there must be some structural influencing of pull and push factors for EDP.
The fourth hypothesis regarding patent application as a measure for pharmaceutical innovations can be mostly confirmed. But further life expectancy only becomes significant if GDP is not included in the estimation equation. This has to be reanalyzed in following research investigations. Still the pharmaceutical industry R&D activity seems to influence patent applications consistently indicating that the same push factor becomes operative. Rising pharmaceutical innovation can lead to increasing healing chances of diseases but it also can lead to rising expenditures in health care. The question is whether in the long run pharmaceutical innovations are able to reduce HCE at all. If pharmaceutical innovations are evidentially effective they can be successful in reducing HCE in short-term but due to rising further life expectancy over the whole life cycle they can result in rising discounted HCE.

The differences of signs for doctors' consultations for HCE and EPD could be an indicator of how effective health care systems are in containing rising EPD. But still the rising of HCE could not be limited in Germany despite individualized drug budgets.

It is true that since the late 1960s the fertility rate declined and finally stabilized on a low level that is not sufficient for the maintenance of population. As a result of the structural change of demography the share of the elderly population demanding social benefits in kind rises. Simultaneously to this development there are changes in attitudes of society towards care for the elderly. A popular impression is that today a greater share of resources is dedicated to dying patients than in the past. To assure a certain level of inter-generational fairness some reforms seem to be in order.

Beside age-related premium rates for health insurances where the insured has to cover its risk herself (Breyer, Zweifel, and Kifmann (2005)), some propose partially capital funded health insurance systems. E.g. Singapore introduced medical savings accounts (MSA) where every individual saves ex ante certain percentages from their gross income. The mandatory character of MSA could offer an alternative to build up a capital stock with the only purpose of using it in case of illness (Eiff, Massaro, Voo, and Ziegenbein (2002)). These kinds of MSA could be used to lessen demand induced rising of HCE.

Finally, ageing population has not to be a problem for society if for instance the society is willing to create additional financial resources in order to cover the rising HCE. Still, the remaining problem seem to be that society has to decide how health care system should be designed and after determining basic parameters it has to operate and really implement the corresponding system by adequate reforms.

Chapter 4

Pharmaceutical Innovations, German Health Care Expenditures, and Mortality

1. Introduction

How do pharmaceutical innovations affect the German health care expenditures and mortality measured as potential years of life lost (PYLL)? Whether technical progress is too expensive or not is not the right question. The point is that R&D has mostly been expensive but nowadays not everything can be paid any longer considering the financial scope of the German health care system. The additional value of pharmaceutical innovation is more and more under scrutiny. Therefore the questions are, how much R&D is necessary and how much R&D can we afford based on the German health care system? This has to be discussed and defined on the social level. To find an optimal resource allocation in the health care system, evidence based cost-benefit analysis is necessary.

In the literature some argue that an ageing population, enlarging medical-technological progress and rising prices inherently cause high future health care expenditures (HCE). Then controlling health care expenditures appears reasonable. This can be done in a lot of different ways on both the demand and supply side. Nevertheless, since 1960 Germany faced a decrease of potential years of life lost (PYLL) of approximately 66 percent and in the same period life expectancy of the total German population increased by about 19 years. As life expectancy is still rising although with a decelerating rate, it could be argued that modern medical progress comes along with diminishing returns. But particularly in countries where the individual willingness-to-pay (WTP) for medical benefits is high as in the US or Switzerland, it can be seen that the share of HCE to social product is also invariably high (Felder (2006)). A high WTP for health care benefits can here alternatively be interpreted as an attempt to reduce the volatility of the further life expectancy.

The objective of this paper is to identify the effects of the main factors on the German PHCE, potential years of life lost, and the approval of new drugs by the German Federal Institute for Drugs and Medical Devices. This will be done by using a vector autoregressive model (VAR) including data for Germany for a period of 19 years (1986-2004). As in previous studies we will examine whether there are structural factors causing continuously rising PHCE and also causing continuously decreasing PYLL. The continuous decrease of PYLL and increase of further life expectancy at age 65 can be interpreted as indicators of overall health improvements. An assessment of this health improvement seems to be difficult. But this kind of assessment is necessary in order to account for different factors. If an extension of life span, which is an indicator of overall health improvement, is translated into concrete gains in economic output, for instance, it is possible to show that each added year increases the national product by 4 percent (Bloom (2001)).

The plan of this paper is as follows. In the next section the influencing factors on pharmaceutical innovations will be identified. The third section considers the impact of pharmaceutical innovations on HCE and the life span taking into consideration previous results as well as a theoretical framework on which the estimation is based on. The fourth section covers the econometric specification and the fifth section presents the estimation results and a short forecast. A forecast period of only four years will be applied in order to produce reliable predictions which are not that sensitive concerning political changes or other influences which are deviating from the implied status quo. Finally, conclusions will be drawn from our analysis.

2. Determinants of Pharmaceutical Innovations

The economic literature distinguishes between three kinds of innovations: process, product, and organizational innovations. Process innovations allow for constant production with less costs, whereas product innovations allow for production of goods with new features or at least new combination of something existing but often causing higher costs. The organizational innovations offer an opportunity to realize lower costs by novel combination of production processes. In the following only product innovations in the pharmaceutical industry will be considered. These pharmaceutical innovations are affected by several important factors, inter alia the legal framework. Changes of the patent law are expected to cause innovation effects on pharmaceuticals. The implementation of the guideline concerning the patentability of biotechnological innovations[1] on the legal protection of biotechnological invention into the German law in 2005 should have had effects on the pharmaceutical market (European Council (1998)).

As biotechnology and genetic engineering are regarded to play an increasingly important role in a broad range of industries, the protection of biotechnological inventions is of fundamental importance for the Community's industrial development. Particular in the field of genetic engineering, R&D requires a considerable amount of high-risk investment and only an adequate legal protection can make them profitable. This does not necessarily mean that a prolongation of the patent protection time should take place. Although incentives such as temporary monopoly profits offered by patent protection seem appropriate to secure a certain R&D level. The Agreement on Trade-Related Aspects of Intellectual Property Rights (TRIPs), which has been signed by all of the member states of the EU, forced the signatories to provide patent protection for products and processes in all areas of technology. The common goal of TRIPs has been to reward inventions or rather innovations. A technological product innovation in this sense comprehends an implemented, technologically new product or a significant technological product improvement. The technological product innovation is implemented if it has been introduced on the market (product innovation). These technical product innovations usually involve a range of scientific, technological, organizational, financial and commercial activities (OECD (1995)). But the concept of implementing something 'new' is emphasized differently according to the different underlying laws. For instance, the patent law stresses the technical aspect of an improvement that has to be significant whereas the social law points out the therapeutical significance of an improvement.

To evaluate additional innovation incentives by the implementation of the directive, Jasper and Trostmann (2005) take into account the dynamics of the biotechnological patent applications in Germany. Clearly, the number of patent applications can not be used to draw conclusions about the quality of the inventions. But using the patent applications as a proxy for the real grant of patents is useful because patent applications and grant of patent run almost parallel. However,

[1] Directive 98/44/EC of the European Commission and Council.

not every patent application fulfills the criteria also to grant a patent and therefore the number of the latter lies between half and one-third of the initial patent applications.

Table 4.1 shows that the numbers of pharmaceutical and biotechnological patent applications are rising continuously. In fact the implementation of the directive clarifies questions concerning the patentability and increases legal certainty. Nevertheless, according to Jasper and Trostmann (2005) the overall innovation effects caused by this directive on the legal protection of biotechnological invention does not lead to essential new R&D impulses because the amended patent law largely incorporates the actual state of the legal practice.

Table 4.1: Number of the pharmaceutical relevant patent applications in Germany

	German		International	
Year	Pharmaceutical	Biotechnological	Pharmaceutical	Biotechnological
	Patent Applications		Patent Applications	
1995	782	65	4,539	645
1996	817	70	4,458	590
1997	917	96	4,987	893
1998	1,153	129	5,568	1,025
1999	1,241	176	6,328	1,214
2000	1,410	183	8,432	1,615
2001	1,446	208	8,619	1,723
2002	1,606	209	9,034	1,779
2003	1,664	247	9,168	1,582

Source: Jasper and Trostmann (2005), p.327.

On the one side a well-known argument of the pharmaceutical industry concerning innovations is that there are no innovations without sufficiently high profit rates of return on pharmaceutical industries' R&D investment. On the other hand the health care insurers argue that without R&D investment by pharmaceutical industry there is no way to gain profits. A pharmaceutical firm is not able to research and develop without investing money. Pharmaceuticals can be seen as competing products and up to a certain degree they are substitute products. And the more innovative they are the less substitutive they become and hence the less competition will be induced. But if pharmaceuticals are substitutes then price-competition among these products will normally follow. Therefore, an innovation can lead to a competitive advantage and thus higher turnovers can be realized. A pharmaceutical industry which is not enough spending on R&D would therefore loose future turnovers.

3. Impact of Pharmaceutical Innovation on HCE and Life Span

3.1. General Arguments

According to Scherer (2001) the relationship between profitability and R&D expenditures can be described in three ways. First, successful R&D leads with a long lag to new products which depending on the market penetration can add greatly to the business profits. Second, realized profits can act as a source of funds to support R&D expenditures. And finally, managers' expectations of future profit opportunities which are anchored by contemporary market conditions can induce a demand-pull influence on R&D expenditures. Scherer (2001) concludes that a stable pattern exists between profit rates of return on pharmaceutical industry R&D investment and risk-adjusted capital cost. Combined with the results that profit rates of return on pharmaceutical industry R&D investment are rather rising above risk-adjusted capital cost even though only by moderate amounts he deduces that a virtuous rent-seeking model is particularly suitable for describing this stable pattern. Barzel (1968) introduced the virtuous rent-seeking model and showed that innovations are induced, since they become more profitable with the expansion of output. However, the resulting amount of resources dedicated to innovating activity would not be optimal. The inability of innovators to appropriate all benefits may tend to make the amount too small. But if the innovations are launched at their optimal dates then their contribution to wealth will be greater than it could have been by the same resources employed elsewhere in the economy. As competition between potential innovators may deprive innovations of all their special economic value, Barzel (1968) concludes that the increasing number of innovations tends to make the R&D spending too large.

A common argument of the pharmaceutical industry is that it needs every day of additional patent protection and market exclusivity so that it is able to use the revenue for future R&D. An interesting question is whether the profits of pharmaceutical industry are a stimulus for R&D and hence pharmaceutical innovations. If so this may result in a range of health-improving pharmaceutical innovations.

But evidences suggest that the flow of drugs to the market in the past five to ten years shows a growing number of innovative drugs which are not superior to existing older drugs (so-called 'me-too drugs').[2] An evaluation whether innovative pharmaceuticals are superior to the pharmaceutical which are already on the market is applied by the Institute for Quality and Efficiency in Health Care (IQWIG). The IQWIG was established in June 2004 to evaluate the quality and efficiency of health care. The Institute's tasks include among others the evaluation of pharmaceuticals following the principles of evidence-based medicine. Taking into account the rising HCE such an evaluation may the play an important role in the attempt to contain HCE.

To interpret how pharmaceutical innovation affects the health care market it is important to specify whether increased pharmaceutical utilization can reduce total HCE. In this case a constraint of pharmaceutical utilization could in some cases increase total HCE. Avorn, Choodnovskiy, MyLaughlin, Ross-Degnan, and Sourmeral (1991) showed that reimbursement caps on pharmaceuticals lead to an approximate doubling of the rate of nursing home admissions among chronically ill elderly patients. But these results are not really unexpected as a crucial factor of chronical illnesses is generally a continuous medication. As patients limit their own medication on the number of reimbursable pharmaceuticals they could receive by their health care insurer they may increase the probability of greater damage to their own health.

Lichtenberg (1998) examined the effect of pharmaceutical innovation on mortality reduction and growth in lifetime per capita income. The results show that in presence of pharmaceutical innovation the further life expectancy and the lifetime income is increasing. Additionally, the author analyzed whether the utilization of newer pharmaceuticals affects the morbidity, the mortality, and the HCE (Lichtenberg (2001)). He founds that patients who are using newer pharmaceuticals namely pharmaceutical innovations are less likely to die by the end of the considered survey and were significantly less likely to experience sick days causing work-loss days than those patients who used older drugs. This study also showed that the use of newer pharmaceuticals tends to reduce all kind of non-pharmaceutical expenditures leading to an overall HCE reduction. For instance, the patients using newer pharmaceuticals had fewer hospital stays than persons consuming older drugs, which leads to the greatest cost containment in this context. But what has not been analyzed in this study is whether the current income affects the use of newer drugs and thus overall HCE and the probability to die at the end of the survey. It is assumable that patients with high incomes are more likely to take steps to

[2] A me-too drug can be described by a marginal molecule variation of existing compounds without necessarily leading to a new therapeutical innovation.

avoid work-loss days since the opportunity costs would be much higher compared to low income patients. But this comparison only stands up if low income patients receive continued remuneration by health care insurance and the opportunity cost of high income patients are more than the pure monetary earnings.

As mentioned above one key question of this paper is how pharmaceutical innovation affects HCE and the life span? Concerning the latter the survival curve can be considered to analyze to which degree the survival rate has changed during the considered period.

Figure 4.1: Survival curves for the German population, 1871-2003

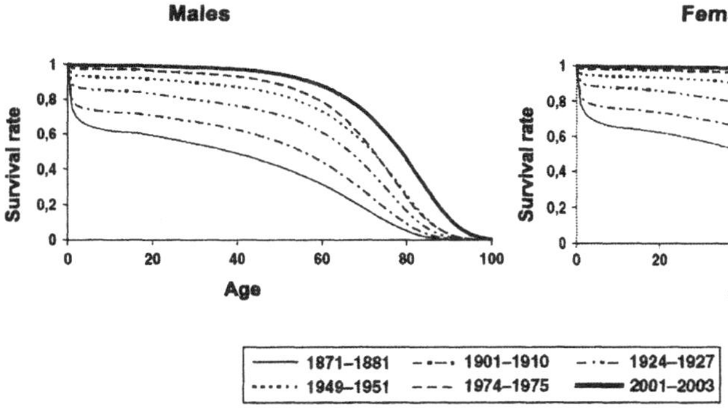

Source: Felder (2006), p. 52.

As Figure 4.1 shows the survival curves changed dramatically in the last century. Due to the decrease of infant mortality the decline of the survival curve at the beginning of the life span has almost totally disappeared. In the course of time death has been banned up to a ripe old age and a rectangularisation of the survival curve can be observed. Hundred years ago in Germany two-third of the population died before reaching the age of 60 and actually the mortality rate of this cohort is under 10 percent. Beside other causes technical progress or rather pharmaceutical progress in the combat of infectious disease for instance caused the rectangularisation of the survival curve. Improved hygiene, enough food, and progresses mainly caused the change of the survival curve. Since then also the medication of cardiovascular diseases makes a fundamental contribution to the increase of the life span.

Table 4.2: Additional gained life years as a result of reduced mortality caused by different selected reasons

Disease	Men			Women		
	1980-1990	1990-2000	Total	1980-1990	1990-2000	Total
Infant mortality	0.59	0.31	0.90	0.43	0.30	0.73
Cardiovascular diseases	0.71	1.41	2.12	0.59	1.22	1.82
Cancer	0.13	0.43	0.55	0.32	0.34	0.66
Metabolism diseases	-0.01	-0.04	-0.05	0.01	0.02	0.02
Accidents	0.36	0.41	0.77	0.32	0.38	0.70
Others	0.22	0.71	0.93	0.08	0.35	0.43
Total	2.00	3.23	5.23	1,75	2.65	4.36

Source: Felder (2006), p. 54.

Table 4.2 shows to which extent the decrease of different causes of death increases the further life expectation. The mortality caused by cardiovascular diseases decreased around one third in the eighties and even 45 percent in the nineties (Felder (2006)). The development of medication concerning infant mortality e.g. against prematurity as tocolytics, cortisone therapy for lung maturation, cardiovascular diseases, cancer e.g. chemo therapy or metabolism diseases e.g. mellitus diabetes which are medicated with pharmaceuticals. Therefore the development of pharmaceuticals has contributed to the increase of further life expectation over all age groups. But obviously the relative prolongation of the residual life span of elderly is shorter compared to younger people as the younger on average are expected to live longer than the elderly. Therefore, the revenue of the health investment has an effect on a much shorter time period considering elderly as they are expected to have a shorter further life expectancy.

Newhouse (1992) analyzed potential factors, for instance ageing, which can be responsible for increasing HCE. He differentiates between factors which affect demand for medical services, such as ageing, the spread of insurance, and the growth of income as well as supply of services such as supplier-induced demand and differential productivity growth[3]. According to his results altogether these factors can explain almost half of the variance. Newhouse (1992) argues that technical progress is the crucial factor to account for the residual increase of HCE.[4] Empirical

[3]According to Baumol (1967) who formulated the cost disease story, labour intensive services show a below average productivity growth. As wage increases in the service sector are geared to the general wage increases which are in turn depending on the general productivity growth, by and by services will be too expensive produced. Assuming inelastic demand for health care services a disproportionate rising of HCE must follow.

[4]Goddeeris (1984), Weisbrod (1991), and Breyer, Zweifel, and Kifmann (2005) made theoretical contributions demonstrating that a larger extent of insurance coverage will tend to result in cost rising product innovations.

evidences for this so-called Newhouse conjecture have been found by Geljins and Rosenberg (1994) and Okunade and Murthy (2002) for most of OECD countries. The prevailing opinion in the literature is that a disproportionate share of the HCE is mainly caused by technical progress. But what can be criticized concerning this widely accepted argument is that preferences remain unconsidered. Without a sufficiently strong demand for medical services the corresponding supply of medical innovations can not be realized, hence both blades of Marshall's scissors are necessary to explain rising HCE (Hall and Jones (2004)). Felder (2006) explains this relation with an economic standard paradigm. If income increases and marginal utility of consumption is decreasing sufficiently strong then the optimal health care expenditure rate will increase over time. Consumption is rising though not as fast as the HCE. The intuition therefore is that with increasing income the value of life is expected to rise. The author argues that, if a person gains wealth, first of all a prolongation of life will be purchased and less additional consumption.[5]
Whether technical innovations in medicine are 'worth it' or not has been analyzed by Cutler and McCellan (2001). The authors analyzed different diseases. They estimated the benefit of pharmaceutical innovations and compared them to their costs. In four (heart attack, low-birthweight infants, depressions, and cataracts) of the five (breast cancer) conditions the estimated benefits of technological innovation are substantially higher than their costs. In the last condition, breast cancer, the benefits and costs are approximately of similar magnitude. Finally, in three of the five conditions pharmaceutical innovations are determined to be valuable.
Additionally, Cutler and McCellan (2001) emphasize that treatment expansion compared to treatment substitution has been neglected in the current research. Pharmaceutical innovation often substitutes for older pharmaceuticals constituting therefore treatment substitution. Whereas if pharmaceutical innovations lead more people to be treated for a disease this can be classified under treatment expansion effect. Cutler and McCellan (2001) conclude that physicians more frequently make a diagnose for a certain disease when the corresponding treatment is safer and easier to realize and patients attend more to their condition when a therapy is more effective. Treatment expansion boosts the costs as it is the case in three of the five cases (depression, cataracts, and breast cancer) but at the same time improves the outcome. This means treatment expansion leads to increasing cost because no therapy other than routine physician visit was provided prior to the diagnosis. In this context the authors argue that some of the greatest suc-

[5]Or to formulate it alternatively: "As we get richer and richer, the most valuable thing we have to purchase is more time to live." Hall and Jones (2004), p. 37.

cesses of the medical care system, and some of the greatest failures, are due to the treatment expansion effect. Although considering these effects would go beyond the scope of this paper, it is clear advisable that treatment expansion effects should attracte more attention in research compared to the past.

3.2. Some Empirical Results of Previous Forecasts

To assess the empirical results it is necessary to consider the underlying assumptions carefully. The status quo hypothesis assumes that with rising further life expectancy also the age-specific health care utilization will relatively increase (Breyer and Felder (2004)). The medicalisation hypothesis implies that, due to the multimorbidity of elderly, increasing further life expectation will result in a greater increase of age-specific health care utilization (Verbrugge (1984)). In this scenario technical progress enables in particular illness prone individuals to survive so that the average state of health in the populations decreases. According to the compression of morbidity hypothesis health care utilization increases because of the proximity to death and not because of the age (Fries (1985)). Longevity leads to higher health care utilization caused by a prolongation of the life span and hence a prolongation of the time period where HCE can occur.

To distinguish the effects of the medical progress and decreasing PYLL it is possible to first analyze the effects of demographic change and then to compare them to forecast results that additionally consider the medical progress. Considering only the pure demographic effects and neglecting cost pressures due to technical progress, Erbsland, Ried, and Ulrich (1999) forecast increasing contribution rates from 12.9 in 1995 to 15.5 in 2040. Breyer and Ulrich (2000) estimate an increase of the health insurance premium rate up to 15.3 in 2040. Whereas Postler's (2003) estimate of the premium rates for the best case is 16.0 percent in 2040. Taking into account these forecast results, the pure demographic effect caused by increasing longevity does not result in dramatically rising contribution rates.

A scenario of Breyer and Ulrich (2000) forecasts of the futures development of expenditures of the German sickness funds assuming that the present institutions remain unchanged. According to the authors previous forecasts which used present age-specific expenditure data are systematically biased as no technical progress is incorporated. To obviate these difficulties, regression analysis is used to separate the factors which are responsible for increasing HCE namely demographic change, rising income and a time trend implemented as an instrumental variable representing medical progress. The prognosis then forecasts increasing premium rates up to 23.1 percent in the year 2040. Also including the effects of technical progress in his worst case scenario, the estimates of Postler (2003) show a premium rate of 32.0 percent in 2040. Only the estimates of PROGNOS (1998) are somewhat unusual. Demographic change and medical progress are incorporated as independent factors. In the first step corresponding HCE based upon the demographic change are estimated and in the next step respective HCE are multiplied with growth factors which should express the technology caused increases in the age groups. Implying that demographic change and technical progress are interdependent this proceeding is not appropriate to cover the effects of both factors. The multiplied growth rates are between 1.2 and 1.7 percent. Comparing these implied growth rates (1.2 or 1.7 percent) with US growth rate from 1985 to 1995 it can be seen that the US growth rate was 3.89 percent which is more than twice as much as the implied German growth rates. Assuming that the German development follows temporally delayed the US development the implied growth rates would be too small (Breyer and Ulrich (2000)). Accordingly, the estimated medical progress effects of PROGNOS (1998) for the year 2040 amounted to only 16.0 percent which is slightly above the calculated effects of the pure demographic effect. Clearly these results show that the contribution rates are more drastically increasing if technical progress is incorporated. However, this brief overview of the various empirical results gives an impression about the rather wide range of the forecasted effects of technical progress for the health care expenditures which may also be an indication of the uncertainty factor of long-term forecasts.

3.3. Theoretical Framework

Within the theoretical framework several assumptions can be made based upon the previous considerations. As the German government has and will spent more and more money for public expenditures on health care (PHCE)[6], it is interesting to determine the effects. As mentioned above PHCE are assumed to interact with the potential years of life lost[7] and the approval of

[6]Public expenditures on health care is defined as health expenditure incurred by public funds. In this context public funds are state, regional and local Government bodies and Social Security Schemes. Public capital formation on health includes publicly financed investment in health facilities plus capital transfers to the private sector for hospital construction and equipment.

[7]The potential years of life lost is a measure of age-specific mortality. The calculation of PYLL involves summing up deaths occurring at each age and multiplying this with the number of remaining years to live up to the selected age limit of 70 years (OECD (2006)).

new drugs. It is assumed that PHCE will increase with previously high PHCE, rising of potential years of life lost as well as rising approval of new drugs. If age-specific death rates are increasing, the public health care expenditures will increase due to costs that occur because more people are in their last year of life[8], and because government will probably take measures to restrict disproportional rising of age-specific mortality rates. Structural effects caused by additional approvals of new drugs are assumed and, therefore, PHCE will increase. For instance, although from 2003 to 2004 a cost reduction of 4.6 billion Euros has been realized, the according decrease in turnovers was only 2.5 billion Euros. This was due to an 18 percent increase of the value per prescription and a 23 percent increase of the structural component caused by introducing new and more expensive pharmaceuticals as well as a 19.9 percent increase of the inter-pharmaceutical effects from non-prescribable towards prescribable pharmaceuticals (Schwabe (2006)).[9]

Decreasing PYLL in the past are assumed to be positive correlated with the current PYLL and thus to result in a decrease of the present PYLL. An increase of public health care expenditures and approvals of new drugs are expected to have negative correlation. This means, if more money is spent in the health care sector it can be assumed that due to a better medical care the potentially lost years will decrease. Or to put it the other way around, a decrease of PYLL should lead to decreasing overall health care expenditures. Additionally, as more new drugs receive the approval more drugs can be prescribed and therefore more diseases can be treated all over the country and this in turn may decrease the age-specific mortality rates.

How high levels of new drug approvals are influencing the current drug approvals is ambiguous. Caused by former frequent new drug approvals it may be that governments try to contain the new approvals because they imply that rising drug approvals increase public health care expenditures. Or on the contrary, frequent drug approval can be an indication for necessity or successful R&D endeavours and therefore former high drug approval would cause future high drug approvals. Implying demand effects, increasing PYLL and PHCE would act as pull factors, since rising of age-specific death rates could cause an increasing demand for new drugs that may be a remedy for the reason of the rising of age-specific death rates. Rising PHCE would

[8]Cross-sectional analysis showed that the increase with age in per capita health care expenditure is primarily attributable to very large expenditure in the last year of life. There are many evidences that the medical costs are considerably rising with increasing proximity to death, for instance Lubitz, Beebe, and Baker (1995) or Zweifel, Felder, and Meier (1996).

[9]These effects are mainly attributable to the Health Care Modernization Act ('Gesundheitsmodernisierungsgesetz', GMG) enacted in 2003.

be an increase of financial incentives that would cause an increasing request of pharmaceutical firms for new drug approvals in order to benefit from the rising public health care expenditures.

4. Econometric Specification

Based upon these theoretical considerations the following empirical implementation of the hypothesis will be examined and forecasts will be applied by using a vector autoregressive model (VAR). In order to gain an impression of the empirical method first an overview of the methodology within the estimation specification will be given.

As vector autoregressions are notably convenient for estimation and forecasting, this method will be applied to analyze the present data according to the following considerations (Hamilton (1994)). A VAR(p) model assumes that there is set of K variables, which are defined as linear functions of p of their own lags and p lags of the other $K-1$ variables. To determine the most appropriate lag-order within a pre-estimation a series of lag-order selection statistics will be applied. In principal, a pth-order VAR model without exogenous variables can be described by:

$$y_t = v + A_1 y_{t-1} + \ldots + A_p y_{t-p} + u_t \quad t \varepsilon \{-\infty, \infty\} \tag{4.1}$$

where $y_t = (y_{1t}, \ldots, y_{Kt})'$ is a $K \times 1$ random vector, the A_i are fixed $K \times K$ matrices of parameters, v is a $K \times 1$ vector of fixed parameters, and u_t is assumed to be white noise; that is, $E(u_t) = 0$, $E(u_t u_t') = \Sigma$, and $E(u_t u_s') = 0$ for $t \neq s$. In order to reduce the number of parameters which have to be estimated, an incomplete VAR(p) is specified. In the case of an incomplete VAR(p) some of the A_i matrices are set to zero (Greene (2003)). Any of the A_i, $i = 1, \ldots, p$ may be zero by simply omitting this certain lag.

The cross-equation error variance-covariance matrix Σ[10] contains all the information about the contemporaneous correlations of implemented VAR(p), which can be the greatest strength and at the same time be the greatest weakness. As no real defeasible a priori assumption are imposed, fitting a VAR(p) equals to let the data speak for themselves. Nevertheless, there have to be imposed some restrictions on the structure of Σ otherwise no causal interpretation of the results can be made.

[10] In the estimation specification instead of the ML divisor $1/T$ an alternative small-sample divisor $1/T - \bar{m}$ is applied, where $\bar{m}$ is the average number of parameters which has been included in each equation.

The distribution of y_t is uniquely determined by the distribution of u_t, and the parameters v and A_i. To estimate the parameters of the VAR(p), as usual, some restrictions on the temporal properties of the distribution of the y_t are necessary. Strictly speaking, the variables in y_t are required to be covariance stationary which means their first two moments exists and are time-invariant. More precisely, a random vector is covariance stationary if $E(z_t)$ is finite and independent of t; $Var(z_t)$ is finite and independent of t; and $Cov(z_t, z_s)$ is a finite function of $|t-s|$ but neither of t nor s.

In the case that u_t have mean of zero, i.i.d. vector process and y_t is covariance stationary and uncorrelated with the disturbance term u_t, then consistent and efficient estimates of the A_i and v can be calculated using seemingly unrelated regression receiving asymptotically normally distributed estimators. If the equations for the variables y_t have the same set of regressors, equation-by-equation OLS estimates are the conditional maximum likelihood estimates (Hamilton (1994)).

According to the prior a VAR(p) with two lags $p = 5, 10$ including the $K = 3$ variables PHCE, PYLL, and APPROV_NEW will be estimated introduction, for the period from 1986 until 2004.[11] The data for this estimation has been pooled by using PHCE and PYLL obtained from the OECD (2006) and APPROV_NEW obtained from the processing statistics of German Federal Insitute for Drugs and Medical Devices (BfArM) (2006). This means the estimation specification contain three linear functions including the two determined lags of period 5 and 10 of the current endogenous variable additionally the same lag-structure of the other $K-1$ variables will be fitted. The following three linear functions will be estimated where $t = 1996, ..., 2004$ and $p = 5, 10$ are defined as follows:

$$PHCE_t = v + \alpha_1 PHCE_{t-p} + \alpha_2 PYLL_{t-p} + \alpha_3 APPROV\_NEW_{t-p} + u_t, \tag{4.2}$$

$$PYLL_t = v + \alpha_1 PHCE_{t-p} + \alpha_2 PYLL_{t-p} + \alpha_3 APPROV\_NEW_{t-p} + u_t, \tag{4.3}$$

$$APPROV\_NEW_t = v + \alpha_1 PHCE_{t-p} + \alpha_2 PYLL_{t-p} + \alpha_3 APPROV\_NEW_{t-p} + u_t. \tag{4.4}$$

[11] The lag order selection statistics for a series of vector autoregressions of order 1,...,maxlag(13) result that VARs of order five and ten are the most appropriated specifications to use. Due to this underlying lag structure the model is using 9 years.

5. Estimation Results and Forecasts

5.1. Pre-Estimation Results

As mentioned above, before running the estimation series of lag-order selection statistics have been applied to determine the optimal lag-order. These statistics report the final prediction error (FPE), Akaike's information criterion (AIC), the Bayesian information criterion (BIC), and the Hannan and Quinn information criterion (HQIC) lag order selection statistics for a series of vector autoregressions of order 1,..,13. These statistics are commonly used to assist in fitting a VAR(p) of the correct order. The FPE has its roots in measuring forecast inaccuracy. Consequently, the VAR(p) with the lowest prediction error is optimal. The FPE resembles the AIC, which means minimization is the goal. But the AIC was initially constructed to measure the differences between the given and the true model. The BIC and the HQIC can be interpreted accordingly to the AIC. Whereas these measures have the advantage that choosing a p that minimize the BIC or the HQIC provides consistent estimates of the true lag order p, while minimizing the AIC or FPE overestimate the true lag order with positive probability (Lütkepohl (1993)). Contrary to the standard model order statistics which include a constant term, an alternative version of information criteria excluding the constant term from the log likelihood has been applied because the exclusion does not affect inference and is recommended by Lütkepohl (1993). A sequence of likelihood-ratio test statistics for all of the VARs of order less than or equal to the highest lag order requested is also reported. These LR-tests are made to determine whether the additional parameters in the VAR, with one additional lag, are zero.[12] The AIC, HQIC, and the BIC chose a model with five lags, whereas the likelihood-ratio test selects a model with ten lags. While fitting the VAR models with five or ten lags, it appeared that these lag-orders seem not to result in a stable model specification therefore a stable model with two lags is implemented.

5.2. Estimation Results

As Table 4.3 shows carrying out the estimation leads to a highly significant model specification. Each of the estimated equation is highly significant.

[12] For an introduction to these statistics see Lütkepohl (1993) and Hamilton (1994).

Table 4.3: VAR results I (Sample: 1996 to 2004)

Equation	Obs	Parms	RMSE	R-sq	F	P
PHCE	9	6	30.4485	0.9999	7303.541	0.0000
PYLL	9	6	75.4735	0.9999	3869.801	0.0000
APPROV_NEW	9	6	55.0085	0.9951	101.5886	0.0015

Also the model lag order statistics depicted in Table 4.4 are relative low as favoured.

Table 4.4: Model lag order selection statistics (Lutstats)

FPE	AIC	HQIC	BIC	LL
1.204e+10	22.383521	21.532301	22.777971	-121.03719

The specific equations including the implemented lag structure of two lags (lag 5 and lag 10) are shown in Table 4.5. The PHCE equation provides positive significant coefficients for the ten periods lagged PHCE (PHCE_L10, $\beta = 0.83$) and APPROV_NEW (APPROV_NEW_L10, $\beta = 0.85$) and marginally positive significant coefficient for the five periods lagged PYLL (PYLL_L5, $\beta = 0.22$). As assumed there is a positive correlation between the PYLL and PHCE. This means a decrease of the lagged endogenous variables PYLL leads to current decreasing PHCE, strictly speaking if age-specific death rates are falling the PHCE are also falling. But if PYLL are rising or stagnating at a high level, government is politically forced to respond to this high PYLL in term of spending more money in the health care market. Alternatively, this is commonly done by investing more money in the current pharmaceutical research sectors. The significant positive long term effects of PHCE_L10 may be an indication of high level of health care coverage or a failure of containing health care expenditures. As in previous studies there are hints for structural components which cause increasing PHCE with increasing presence of pharmaceuticals (Ilgin and Eisen (2007)). The PYLL equation becomes hardly significant. Only PYLL_L5 has a positive significant effect with a coefficient of 0.89 indicating that changes in PYLL take place rather slowly. These results are in line with the expected interactions discussed in the section 3.2. The APPROV_NEW equation captures significant short term and long term effects. The significant short term effects by increasing PHCE_L5 ($\beta = 1.31$) lead to a disproportionate high increase of the current APPROVE_NEW evidencing a supply side effect of the pharmaceutical firms for new drug approvals with the objective to benefit from rising public health care expenditures. Whereas increasing PYLL_L5 ($\beta = -0.50$) leads to an unexpected decrease of the current APPROVE_NEW which may be due to a longer necessary R&D lag to produce drugs in order to reduce specific mortality rates. The significant negative long term effects of PHCE_L10 ($\beta = -1.66$) leads to a disproportionate decrease of the current APPROVE_NEW which could be due to cost containment attempts of the German government. The long term effects of PYLL_L10 are marginally significant and positive evidencing an expected demand effect as former high PYLL would interact as a pull factor because rising age-specific death rates would cause an increasing demand for new drugs that may be a remedy for the reasons of high PYLL.

Table 4.5: VAR results II

		Coef.	Std. Err.	t	$P > \|t\|$	[95% Conf. Interval]	
PHCE							
PHCE	L5	.0265338	.2218457	0.12	0.912	-.6794783	.732546
	L10	.8313789	.2238124	3.71	0.034	.1191078	1.54365
PYLL	L5	.2195157	.0858834	2.56	0.084	-.0538037	.4928351
	L10	-.0527127	.1039472	-0.51	0.647	-.3835192	.2780938
APPROV_NEW	L5	.1558594	.2647484	0.59	0.597	-.6866884	.9984071
	L10	.8450729	.2553238	3.31	0.045	.0325188	1.657627
PYLL							
PHCE	L5	-.6301734	.5498942	-1.15	0.335	-2.380182	1.119835
	L10	.543195	.5547691	0.98	0.400	-1.222328	2.308718
PYLL	L5	.8911944	.2128812	4.19	0.025	.2137112	1.568678
	L10	.0281644	.2576564	0.11	0.920	-.7918134	.8481422
APPROV_NEW	L5	-.313327	.6562382	-0.48	0.666	-2.40177	1.775116
	L10	.8955019	.632877	1.41	0.252	-1.118595	2.909599
APPROV_NEW							
PHCE	L5	1.310922	.4007881	3.27	0.047	.0354354	2.586408
	L10	-1.658949	.4043412	-4.10	0.026	-2.945743	-.3721546
PYLL	L5	-.5008835	.1551576	-3.23	0.048	-.9946643	-.0071028
	L10	.5149445	.1877918	2.74	0.071	-.0826928	1.112582
APPROV_NEW	L5	.8514998	.4782964	1.78	0.173	-.6706529	2.373653
	L10	-.9635437	.4612697	-2.09	0.128	-2.43151	.5044225

5.3. Post-Estimation Results

After applying a VAR, and before proceeding with the interpretation and forecasting, it is advisable to control for the fitting underlying data of the VAR. Proceeding this way the FPE now chooses a model with two lags but still the AIC, HQIC, BIC choose a model with five lags. A Granger-causality Wald test, a technique for determining whether one time series is useful in forecasting another, is applied (Hamilton (1994)). I.e. Granger-causality means that values of one time series provide statistically significant information on forecasted values of another time series. As shown in Table 4.6 Granger-causality is given for the PHCE equation itself ($p = 0.0174$) and PHCE Granger-cause APPROV_NEW ($p = 0.0111$) and marginally PYLL ($p = 0.0992$). But Granger-causality is not given for none of the other equations. The Wald test provides significant effects for the APPROV_NEW equation itself ($p = 0.0281$) and marginally significant effects for the PYLL equation ($p = 0.0558$) and the PHCE equation ($p = 0.0880$).

Table 4.6: Granger causality Wald tests

Equation	Excluded	F	df	df_r	$Prob > F$
PHCE	PYLL	28.5711	2	3	0.0111
PHCE	APPROV_NEW	5.4979	2	3	0.0992
PHCE	ALL	19.5145	4	3	0.0174
PYLL	PHCE	0.6608	2	3	0.5784
PYLL	APPROV_NEW	1.2109	2	3	0.4116
PYLL	ALL	0.7363	4	3	0.6248
APPROV_NEW	PHCE	8.7705	2	3	0.0558
APPROV_NEW	PYLL	6.0837	2	3	0.0880
APPROV_NEW	ALL	13.8814	4	3	0.0281

Figure 4.2 shows the orthogonalised impulse-response function. After fitting a VAR it is advisable to estimate series of impulse-response functions (IRF) by bootstrapping the residuals in order to describe how innovations $(\varepsilon_{1t},\ldots,\varepsilon_{nt})$ to one variable influences another variable after a given number of periods. The orthogonalised IRF is based on decomposing the initial VAR innovations $(\varepsilon_{1t},\ldots,\varepsilon_{nt})$ into a set of uncorrelated components $(u_{1t},\ldots,u_{nt})$ and computing the consequences for the prospective y_{t+s} of a unit impulse in u_{it} holding everything else constant (Hamilton (1994)).

Figure 4.2: Orthogonalised impulse-response function*

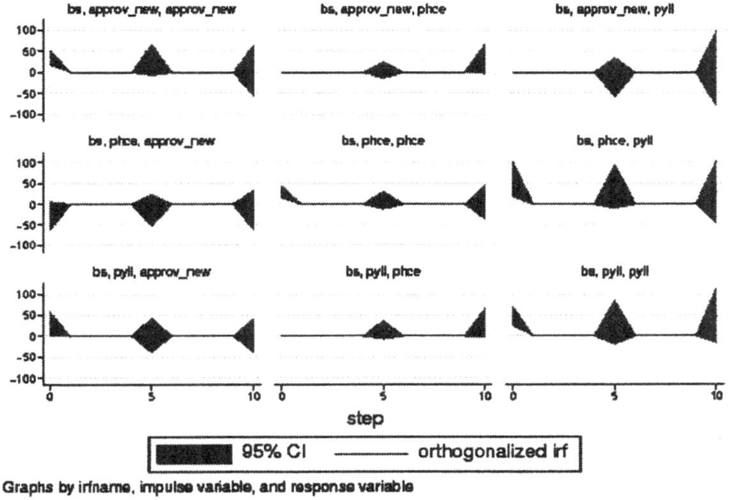

Source: author's own estimation

*Standard errors of the estimated functions are obtained by bootstrapping (bs) the residuals.

Continuation on the next page.

Table 4.7: Eigenvalue stability condition

Eigenvalue		Modulus
-.9021572	+ .13364491	.91200246
-.9021572	- .13364491	.91200246
-.8464403	+ .50632406	.98631906
-.8464403	- .50632406	.98631906
-.7431072	+ .64854985	.98631906
-.7431072	- .64854985	.98631906
-.7508691	+ .54553833	.92812525
-.7508691	- .54553833	.92812525
-.4058858	+ .81670389	.91200246
-.4058858	- .81670389	.91200246
-.64899	+ .47151886	.8021958
-.64899	- .47151886	.8021958
-.151678	+ .89930099	.91200246
-.151678	- .89930099	.91200246
.2199784	+ .96147533	.98631906
.2199784	- .96147533	.98631906
.3871748	+ .90714991	.98631906
.3871748	- .90714991	.98631906
.2868065	+ .88269956	.92812525
.2868065	- .88269956	.92812525
.2478921	+ .76293355	.8021958
.2478921	- .76293355	.8021958
.651306	+ .63839567	.91200246
.651306	- .63839567	.91200246
.808415	+ .42215367	.91200246
.808415	- .42215367	.91200246
.9823944	+ .08790037	.98631906
.9823944	- .08790037	.98631906
.9281252		.92812525
.8021958		.8021958

All the eigenvalues lie inside the unit circle.
VAR satisfies stability condition.

Table 4.7 shows that the necessary eigenvalue stability condition is given and the fitted VAR satisfies the stability conditions. Therefore, an informative interpretation of the orthogonalised impulse functions and the following forecast-error variance decomposition is possible.

Table 4.8: Augmented Dickey-Fuller test of unit roots*

DF-GLS for phce (no. of obs =25)		Maxlag = 9 chosen by Schwert criterion		
	DF-GLS tau	1% Critical	5% Critical	10% Critical
(lags)	Test Statistic	Value	Value	Value
9	-0.722	-3.770	-2.779	-2.377
8	-0.788	-3.770	-2.775	-2.407
7	-1.585	-3.770	-2.812	-2.468
6	-1.374	-3.770	-2.882	-2.552
5	-1.100	-3.770	-2.975	-2.652
4	-1.628	-3.770	-3.081	-2.759
3	-1.269	-3.770	-3.191	-2.866
2	-1.641	-3.770	-3.296	-2.965
1	-2.384	-3.770	-3.386	-3.049
Min SC = 7.678504 at lag 1 with RMSE 40.87411				
Min MAIC = 7.755656 at lag 8 with RMSE 31.11105				

DF-GLS for pyll (no. of obs =35)		Maxlag = 9 chosen by Schwert criterion		
	DF-GLS tau	1% Critical	5% Critical	10% Critical
(lags)	Test Statistic	Value	Value	Value
9	-1.689	-3.770	-2.714	-2.405
8	-1.364	-3.770	-2.771	-2.471
7	-1.594	-3.770	-2.840	-2.543
6	-1.640	-3.770	-2.915	-2.619
5	-2.179	-3.770	-2.993	-2.697
4	-2.012	-3.770	-3.072	-2.772
3	-1.830	-3.770	-3.147	-2.843
2	-1.460	-3.770	-3.215	-2.906
1	-1.206	-3.770	-3.273	-2.960
Min SC = 10.09214 & Min MAIC = 10.04053 at lag 1 with RMSE 140.3993				

DF-GLS for approv_new (no. of obs =11)		Maxlag = 7 chosen by Schwert criterion		
	DF-GLS tau	1% Critical	5% Critical	10% Critical
(lags)	Test Statistic	Value	Value	Value
7	-0.651	-3.770	-4.929	-3.642
6	-0.382	-3.770	-3.828	-2.861
5	-0.362	-3.770	-3.218	-2.467
4	-0.629	-3.770	-2.989	-2.368
3	-1.675	-3.770	-3.030	-2.474
2	-1.981	-3.770	-3.229	-2.692
1	-1.929	-3.770	-3.476	-2.932
Min SC = 9.747185 & Min MAIC = 10.85015 at lag 1 with RMSE 105.1725				

* Opt Lag (Ng-Perron seq t) = 0 [use maxlag(0)]

Table 4.8 shows the augmented Dickey-Fuller (DF) GLS regression testing for a unit root on a time series. If the DF-GLS tau test statistic Z(t) exceeds the critical values, the null of unit root is rejected for the current lag. But since the DF-GLS tau test statistic Z(t) in the current sample never exceeds the critical value, for all the chosen lags the null of an unit root can not be rejected for none of the variables.[13]

Table 4.9: Wald test

1. Equation: PHCE

Lag	F	df	df_r	*Prob* > *F*
5	2.364	3	3	0.249
10	8.435	3	3	0.057

2. Equation: PYLL

Lag	F	df	df_r	*Prob* > *F*
5	8.638	3	3	0.055
10	0.997	3	3	0.501

3. Equation: APPROV_NEW

Lag	F	df	df_r	*Prob* > *F*
5	11.184	3	3	0.039
10	12.526	3	3	0.033

4. Equation: ALL

Lag	F	df	df_r	*Prob* > *F*
5	18.835	9	3	0.017
10	6.713	9	3	0.072

A Wald test is computed to check for each equation and for all equations jointly whether all the endogenous variables of a given lag are jointly zero. As the VAR was fitted with a small sample option, the Wald test statistics provides small-sample F statistics. Table 4.9 shows that the first and second equations (PHCE, PYLL) may have different lag structures than the third and fourth equation considering all equations jointly (APPROV_NEW, ALL). For the first and second equation it is not possible to reject the null hypothesis that all three endogenous variables have zero coefficients at the first lag for the PHCE equation and at the second lag for the PYLL equation. However, the hypothesis that all three endogenous variables of the APPROVE_NEW and ALL equation have zero coefficients at the first or second lag can be rejected at the 5 percent level.

[13]The post-estimation analysis of the VAR model is performed under the assumption that the disturbances are not autocorrelated. The Lagrange multiplier test statistics for the residual autocorrelation results that the exogenous variables are collinear with the dependent variable. Taking the logarithm of the monetary data (PHCE) was no remedy for collinearity nor was taking the logarithm of all of the variables or squaring the proxy for pharmaceutical innovation a remedy. This data transformation only yield in worse estimation results and instability of the eigenvalues.

Table 4.10: Normality test

Jarque-Bera results				
Equation		Chi2	df	*Prob > chi2*
PHCE		2.7870	2	0.24821
PYLL		2.9404	2	0.22988
APPROV_NEW		2.9011	2	0.23444
ALL		8.6284	6	0.19558
Skewness results				
Equation	Skewness	Chi2	df	*Prob > chi2*
PHCE	-0.1901	0.0542	1	0.81588
PYLL	0.0684	0.0070	1	0.93326
APPROV_NEW	0.0488	0.0036	1	0.95234
ALL	.	0.0648	3	0.99570
Kurtosis results				
Equation	Kurtosis	Chi2	df	*Prob > chi2*
PHCE	0.3005	2.7328	1	0.09831
PYLL	0.2032	2.9334	1	0.08677
APPROV_NEW	0.2203	2.8975	1	0.08872
ALL	.	8.5636	3	0.03569

Table 4.10 shows the results of a series of test statistics against the null hypothesis that the disturbances are not normally distributed. The test statistics are applied on the orthogonalised VAR residuals. Neither the single-equation Jarque-Bera statistics nor the joint Jarque-Bera statistic come close to rejecting the null hypothesis of normally distributed residuals. The Jarque-Bera test are obtained by considering the sum of the skewness and the kurtosis statistics.[14] As all these post-estimation procedures have been applied after fitting the VAR, the next section will consider the short term forecast that have been carried out.

5.4. Forecast

An advantage of fitting a VAR is that it is possible to obtain predictions. Specifying equation (1) and defining a VAR(p) including only endogenous variables as determined above we obtain

$$y_t = \nu + A_1 y_{t-1} + \dots + A_p y_{t-p} + u_t. \tag{4.5}$$

[14] For more detailed information see Lütkepohl (1993).

A dynamical prediction of the variables in the vector y_t conditional on the p initial values of the endogenous variable will be carried out, the optimal h-step ahead forecast of y_{t+h} adopting the notation of Lütkepohl (1993, p.83) can be written as

$$\hat{y}_t = \hat{\nu} + \hat{A}_1 y_{t-1} + \ldots + \hat{A}_p y_{t-p}, \tag{4.6}$$

where $\hat{y}_t \equiv y_{t+j}$ for $j \leq 0$. The asymptotic confidence bounds can be estimated because no exogenous variables are considered. Forecasting and parameter estimation are based on independent processes with identical stochastic structure. According to Lütkepohl (1993), the asymptotic estimator of the covariance matrix of the predictors then is given by the MSE (Mean Squared Error) and forecast-error correction term

$$\hat{\Sigma}_{\hat{y}}(h) = \hat{\Sigma}_y(h) + \frac{1}{T}\hat{\Omega}(h). \tag{4.7}$$

$\hat{\Sigma}_y(h)$ is the estimated MSE of the forecast and estimates the forecast-error due to the unseen innovations. $\frac{1}{T}\hat{\Omega}(h)$ estimates the error in the forecast caused by using estimated coefficients instead of the true coefficients.[15] The larger the sample becomes the closer $\frac{1}{T}\hat{\Omega}(h)$ will be to zero. As assumed and evidenced that y_t is normally distributed, the confidence interval for the forecast of y_t covering a h period ahead can be written as

$$\hat{y}_{k,t}(h) \pm z_{\frac{\alpha}{2}} \hat{\sigma}_k(h), \tag{4.8}$$

where $\hat{\sigma}_k(h)$ is the kth diagonal element of $\hat{\Sigma}_{\hat{y}}(h)$. The estimated standard errors, depicted in Figure 4.3, are obtained by simulations with 2500 repetitions using bootstrapped residuals.
It is true that since the poor forecasting performance of certain occurrences in the past, e.g. the oil price shocks due to the OPEC oil embargoes in 1973 or 1979, the glamour of forecasting models has been subsided. In this context the so-called Lucas critique is particulary known. It says that is parameters which are estimated from an econometric model are dependent on the prevailing policy at the time the model was estimated and are very likely to change if the current policy changes (Lucas (1976)). Consequently the estimated parameters are time variant in the presence of policy changes. In order to account for this only a rather short run prognosis has been applied, resulting in plausible results.

[15] $\hat{\Sigma}_y(h)$ is defined as $E[y_{t+h} - y_t(h)][y_{t+h} - y_t(h)]' = \sum_{i=0}^{h-1} \hat{\Phi}_i \hat{\Sigma} \hat{\Phi}_i$. For more detailed information see Lütkepohl (1993), p. 177-178.

Figure 4.3: Forecast for 4 years with 2500 repetitions*

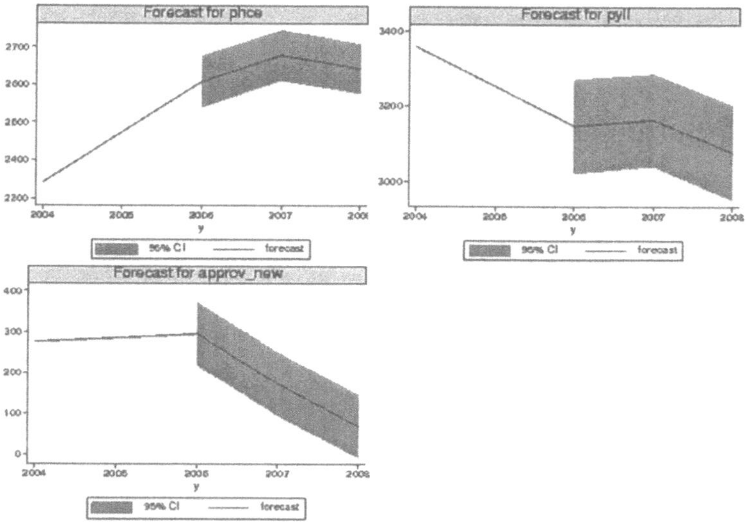

Source: author's own estimation

*Standard errors of the estimated functions are obtained by bootstrapping (bs) the residuals.

This short term forecast period of four years has been chosen to obtain reliable prediction which are not expected to be influenced by changes in politics for instance. The commonly applied long term prediction (up to 2040) are not straightforward to assess. Considering a forecast period of 30 years it appears difficult to believe that researchers are able to incorporate the unforeseen developments in politics, demographic change or rather technological progress. Therefore, the specified forecast period will be only four years in order to produce reliable predictions which are not that sensitive concerning technical progress or other influences which are deviating from the implied status quo.

The forecast of the public health care expenditures shows that although the PHCE still rises, the increase is rather modest considering the past development of the PHCE in the previous years in the sample starting from 1106 US$[16] in 1986 to 2341 US$ in 2004. For 2008 even a slight decrease from 2679 US$ to 2643 US$ in 2009 is forecasted. The PYLL are also expected to de-

[16]The PHCE are given in US$ Purchasing Power Parity (PPP), per capita.

crease slightly. The forecast which has been carried out for APPROV_NEW indicates a rather strong decline. However the predicted new drug approval in 2006 of 295 is a good prognosis of the real drug approval which was in fact 292.

6. Implications and Conclusions

How do pharmaceutical innovations affect the German public health care expenditures and the potential years of life lost? The empirical analysis undertaken in this study indicates that increasing pharmaceutical innovations instrumented as new drug approvals cause a long term effect of rising public health care expenditures. Whereas in the short run rising public health care expenditures seem to create incentives for increasing pharmaceutical innovation, in the long run this relationship turns into the opposite direction and causes an decrease of pharmaceutical innovations. The reason for this might be that in the short run the demand induced effect is causing a positive relationship between public health care expenditures and pharmaceutical innovations instrumented as new drug approvals. But as the drug approvals increase potentially due to rising profit opportunities in the long run, a substitution effect takes place where government tries to contain rising expenditures on pharmaceuticals. As expected this substitution effect takes place in the long run because the regulative measures of governments and the prescribing behaviours of physicians tend to react temporally delayed.

There could not be found any evidence that the pharmaceutical innovations influence potential years of life lost. In fact, I did expect that the drug approvals affect mortality. The reason why this does not take place might be due to different reasons. The variable new drug approval is rather broadly defined and does not only capture ageing specific new drug approvals. Additionally, the measure PYLL depends on many factors. The age-specific mortality rates included in the variable PYLL are limited up to 70 years. It is also quite conceivable that PYLL is affected by medico-technical progress such as improved surgeries.

But what has been found is that decreasing lagged potential years of life lost reduce the public health care expenditures. This is insofar an interesting aspect as the PYLL are falling in the past and are forecasted to decrease continuously. As shown in previous studies (Avorn, Choodnovskiy, MyLaughlin, Ross-Degnan, and Sourmeral (1991); Lichtenberg (1998); Lichtenberg (2001)) pharmaceutical innovations are reducing mortality and this again reduces the overall

HCE, in this study there has been found evidence that decreasing PYLL reduce the German public health care expenditures. This result does not support the medicalisation hypothesis of an disproportional increase of HCE due to multimorbidity (Verbrugge (1984)). The results are rather consistent with the status quo hypothesis of a proportional increase with rising share of the elderly (Breyer and Felder (2004)). What can not be determined strictly is whether this relationship would be different if the PYLL age limit specified by the OECD would be higher then 70 years. For this a re-analysis should be applied in order to incorporate this kind of uncertainty sources.

Additionally, there is evidence that the public health care expenditures influence the R&D level negatively in the long run. Given the essential role that R&D plays in economic growth and welfare, it seems necessary that prospective analyzes should be undertaken capturing the effects of policy changes on R&D activities in the pharmaceutical industry.

It is important to analyze whether the public health care costs are increasing with rising new drug approvals. If more drug approvals increase the overall health care expenditures then past innovation may have enhanced quality but was not successful in containing costs. It could be seen from the data, rising HCE are a reason for increasing endeavour to produce more new drug approvals in order to profit from this attractive health care market. If these kinds of incentives are given then it must also be possible to alter incentives for medical innovations toward the development of cost-reducing technologies. At the same time it is true that there are difficulties in creating politically right incentives without reducing incentives for innovation. By creating a cost-consciousness for rising health care expenditures this inevitably rises the question about priorities among research categories and the extend of the health insurance service catalogue results. Given the uncertainties in R&D it is difficult to determine categories that offer the best prospects for cost containing new technologies. Still how innovations finally will affect costs depends on the manner in which they are implemented into the larger system of medical care and how physicians and patients make use of it. Finally, the findings suggest the need for future research to invest more efforts in conceptualizing, measuring and considering the effects of pharmaceutical innovations in their econometric modeling of increasing health care expenditures.

Chapter 5

Summing up - Pharmaceutical Innovation and Ageing: Some Conclusions and Implications for the Health Care Market

1. Introduction

Health spending continues to increase in OECD countries and if this current trends persist, government will need to rise taxes, cut spending in other areas or make people pay more out of the own pocket in order to maintain the prevailing health care systems (OECD (2006)). Therefore, financing the Social Health Insurance (henceforth: SHI) in the future is commonly assumed to be one of the major problems in the actual health care debate considering rising health care expenditures. Using the contribution rates as an indicator for the development of the current HCE, in 2006, the average contribution in the German SHI was 13.32 percent (Bundesministerium für Gesundheit (2007)). To gain an impression of the future development of the cost structure of the SHI usually forecasts are applied. In fact, there have been numerous contributions to forecast the future development of the contribution rates of the German sickness funds. The forecasted margins are rather wide.

Examining only ageing effects and neglecting cost pressure due to technical progress Breyer and Ulrich's (2000) estimate of the health insurance premium rate is 15.3 in 2040. In contrast, Postler's (2003) estimate of the premium rate for the best case is 16.0 in 2040. Taking into account these forecast results, the pure demographic effects caused by increasing longevity and reduced reproduction rates does not result in dramatically rising contribution rates.

However, including the effects of technical progress the estimates of Postler (2003) show in his worst case scenario a premium rate of 32 percent in 2040.

As a consequence to this variance there is a big uncertainty about the future development of the HCE mainly due to medical progress and ageing which is usually assumed to affect the demand structure of health care services. Additionally, some experts assume that, because benefits are predominantly in kind rather than cash, this will add another uncertainty to the increasing demand for health care services due to the demographic change (Breyer and Felder (2004)). As a result of these uncertainties some argue that, to finance the health care systems in the long run, fundamental reforms are necessary. Usually, to contain the rising health care costs rationalization as well as rationing are discussed (Breyer (2000)).

For the SHI systems this means that governments have strong vested interests to concentrate on the short-run goal of containing the health care budget. Still governments have also incentives to support pharmaceutical firms with respect to their innovation costs by granting them monopoly rights by means of patents for example. It should also be mentioned that the production sector of pharmaceuticals is an important growth sector in many industrialized countries. Furthermore, the pharmaceutical market is an important component of the health care market but has never been scrutinized with respect to ageing.

Figure 5.1: Expenditures in the SHI system 2005 (in percent)

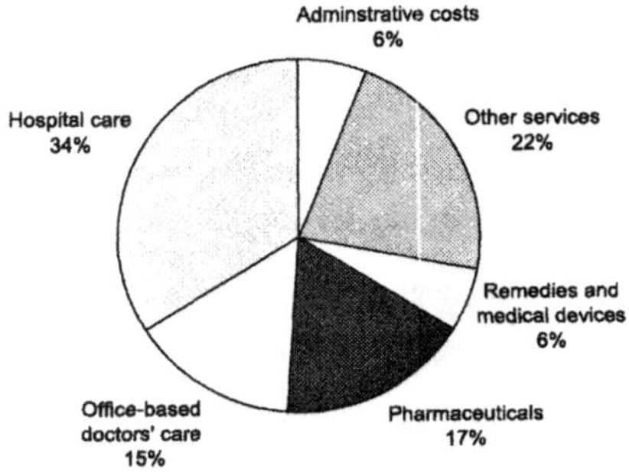

Source: VFA (2006), p. 37.

As Figure 5.1 shows expenditures on pharmaceuticals are the third largest cost component of the expenditures in the SHI. In order to close this gap the foregone studies (Eisen and Ilgin (2007), Ilgin and Eisen (2007), and Ilgin (2007)) focused on the pharmaceutical market, particularly on the aspect of how pharmaceutical innovations and ageing interact.
To give considerations to these thoughts this chapter is structured as follows. Section 2 reviews previous results of the way in which demographic change and pharmaceutical innovation may affect the HCE and expenditures on pharmaceuticals. In section 3 some conclusions will be drawn. Finally, in section 4, political implications will be given.

2. Previous Results

Based upon previous thoughts several assumptions have been analyzed concerning the relation of medical progress and ageing. To examine this relationship an international and a national study have been conducted. The instrumentation of medical progress and ageing has been varied within the two studies. In order to consider supply and demand components different regressors are taken into account. Ageing is measured either as the share of 65+, the further life expectancy at age 65 or the potential years of life lost which act as demand components or rather pull factors of expenditures on prescribed drugs (EPD). The medical progress is measured either as innovations or new drug approvals. The R&D expenditures of pharmaceutical industry and health care utilization measured as doctors' consultations cover the supply components or rather push factors of EPD and innovations.
According to the a priori hypotheses it is assumed that increasing push and pull factors will cause rising EPD and innovations. For instance, increasing ageing leads to growing HCE and EPD. Rising R&D or medical progress inducing activity of pharmaceutical industry will cause a supply induced increase of EPD but decreasing HCE because of a substitution effect between innovative drugs and more expensive medical technology such as a surgery. As intensified R&D activity of pharmaceutical industry will cause an increase of innovative drugs that will be patented and therefore necessarily be prescribed, expenditures on over-the-counter drugs (EOD) should not be affected by this kind of innovative activity. The underlying assumption is that pharmaceutical industry is particularly interested in innovative medicines for dominating health problems of elderly which are mostly chronic diseases, in particular cardiovascular,

metabolic, muscle and skeleton disease, oncological diseases as malignant growth, and psychological diseases for instance dementia and depressions.

In fact, results showed that the mentioned pull and push factors induce rising HCE. Concerning the EPD, the R&D expenditures of pharmaceutical industry and a rising share of 65+ increases EPD. In accordance with prior assumptions there are no effects on the EOD besides EOD of previous years. The pharmaceutical innovations rose with increasing further life expectancy at age 65 and R&D expenditures of the pharmaceutical industry. Results also showed that HCE of prior years had significant negative effects on the current HCE. This can be explained by the endeavour of countries to contain HCE. Viewing the moving average growth rates of HCE, in fact, after several years of rising HCE each of the considered countries faced a reduction of the moving average growth rates in the following years and then again HCE continued to increase. For instance, in Finland, 1991 and 1992 the moving average growth rates of HCE first decreased and then increased again for the following three years and then decreased. The development of EPD is based on the same principle which means that governments search for possibilities to contain EPD. Again, this can be seen in the data including the moving average growth rates of EPD.

The health care utilization has different effects on HCE and EPD. Increasing doctors' consultations lead to increasing HCE which can be due to following up therapies. But increasing doctors' consultations lead to decreasing EPD. Increasing health care utilization results in rising HCE and declining EDP. This can be caused by successful application of lower medical therapies or also by additional following up non-medical therapies which are not affecting EPD.

Results also confirmed that increasing pharmaceutical industry activity in the current period as well as the further life expectancy at age 65 lead to increasing innovations measured as patent applications. Examining the data for the R&D expenditures none of the countries faced continuous rising growth rates for R&D expenditures which can be due to the different political and economical developments in the considered countries. Nevertheless, R&D expenditures of the pharmaceutical industry have relative strong effect onto the size of patent applications.

The international analysis showed that rising pharmaceutical innovations lead to increasing further life expectancy at age 65. This means that pharmaceutical innovations are de facto reducing the mortality rate or in other words are life prolonging. Unfortunately, the national analysis did not reveal this kind of relationship for Germany. The reason why the new drug approvals did not affect the mortality rate can have various reasons. For instance, the variable new drug approval is rather broadly defined and does not only capture ageing specific new drug approvals. Additionally, the ageing measure of potential years of life lost depends on many factors. The age-specific mortality rates included in the variable potential years of life lost are limited up to 70 years. And it is also easily conceivable that potential years of life lost are affected by medico-technical progress such as improved surgeries. But national analysis showed increasing long-term HCE with rising new drug approvals and increasing short-term HCE with rising mortality. In the short-term the approval of new drugs increases with rising HCE, but the long-term approval of new drugs decreases with rising HCE and increases with rising mortality. These results reveal the long-term cost containment strategies of the German government concerning rising HCE due to seemingly innovative drugs (so-called 'me-too drugs') that are not be proven to be superior to existing older drugs. Additionally, rising mortality provides incentives to reduce mortality by innovating new drugs. After reviewing these previous results of the international and national analyzes, in the next section some conclusions will be drawn in order to derive political implications for the last section.

3. Conclusions

Considering the pull and push effects causing increases in HCE, it seems inevitable that HCE will continue to rise. If government try to contain the costs there are different measures imaginable. Usually rationalization and rationing are discussed in this context. A relevant question is, whether reforms of the organization and the reward system in the health care market are effective enough. Or whether stronger rationing is necessary to contain rising costs? To some extent rationing has already been applied in the German SHI insofar as lifestyle drugs that mainly enhance the private lifestyle, e.g. Viagra, are not paid any longer by the SHI.

To evaluate the innovativeness of new drugs there are different measures applied in the EU. For instance, in France the ASMR (Amélioration du Service Médical Rendu) evaluation is applied. In the UK the National Institute of Clinical Excellence (NICE) plays a crucial role for the evaluation of medical innovations. In Germany the new Institute for Quality and Efficiency in Health Care ('Institut für Qualität und Wirtschaftlichkeit im Gesundheitswesen (IQWIG)') undertakes these tasks. The IQWIG is an independent scientific institute that evaluates the quality and efficiency of health care and can be interpreted as a kind of 'evaluated rationing'. The IQWIG investigates what therapeutic and diagnostic services are feasible and valuable. The specific department of drug assessment primarily undertakes commissions on the evaluation of the benefits and harms of pharmaceuticals, which are awarded by the Federal Joint Committee ('Gemeinsamer Bundesausschuss (GBA)') or the Federal Ministry of Health ('Bundesministerium für Gesundheit (BMG)'). The Institutes' objectives include evidence-based medicine and methods for the risk-benefit assessment of pharmaceuticals with the aim to determine whether pharmaceuticals are actually more beneficial than harmful to a patient in the long term. If pharmaceuticals are not more beneficial the Federal Joint Committee excludes pharmaceuticals from the list of services covered by the SHI. An advantage of this explicit rationing depending on transparent criteria of IQWIG is that risk averse patients have the opportunity to take out a complementary insurance for those benefits which are not covered by the SHI. Additionally, the health care reform ('GKV-Wettbewerbstärkungsgesetz (GKV-WSG)') in 2007 widened the commission of IQWIG in view of rationalization insofar that the Institute examines whether prices of pharmaceuticals have an adequate cost-benefit ratio in a therapeutical sense. Taking into account the rising HCE it is advisable to implement such a cost-benefit measure to determine those innovative pharmaceuticals that are really superior to existing pharmaceuticals.

Based on the desire of enhancing the individual state of health up to old-age one should add that individuals also try to regulate their state of health in term of reducing the volatility around a certain reference value (Zweifel (2001)). It is true that individuals can not choose their time of death but they have strong incentives to prolong their life span. Since the further life expectancy is continuously rising in industrialized countries this development can be interpreted as a consequence of individual endeavours to prolongate life span. If this is true then governments are not confronted with an uncontrolled 'obsolescence' of society but rather with intended individual actions that they will be hardly argued out of doing so.

Additionally, it should be mentioned that women will have 70 of 77 years of active life expectancy at birth and this increase is equivalent to gains in terms of further active life expectancy (Cambois and Robine (1996)). Regarding longevity as a target-oriented behaviour of the whole society then it is necessary to reconsider to what extent government should satisfy these demands within the limits of a financially feasible SHI. Or the communication should head for where ageing and technical progress is not overemphasised but is desired by society.

The future income of the German SHI mainly depends on the pre-tax payroll and the growth of the number of persons employed, the unemployment rate, still the non-contributory dependent coverage, and the change of the retirees´ quota. Some argue that if the premium rates are continuously increasing in the next decades then the future employed population will be burdened with a disproportional inter-generational high financing cost (Erbsland, Ried, and Ulrich (1999)). Therefore, discussions concerning the extent of the services covered by the SHI should be taken up in order to find a satisfying consensus. Hence in the next section political implication will be discussed how to approach this problem.

4. Political Implications

In this section different political recommendations will be introduced. Some of them have been already implemented and some of them should be discussed and put into practice if they are chosen to be suitable.

Information Management

Since many problems in the health insurance market originate from asymmetric information, improving the communication is a relevant aspect in the health care market. For instance, health insurance funds could provide risk information which enables their insurees to evaluate the trade-off between health and other goals in life (Zweifel (2000)). According to the information, insurees could be able to choose the optimal health insurance contract or they could simply change their behaviour. It should not be a problem to inform the insurees about the most probable diseases. Communication also takes place between patients and physicians. Therefore, physicians are also in the position to furnish their patients with valuable information, for instance, about which physical subsystem will fail the soonest. If respiratory disease will fail soonest the patient could take preventive measures to avoid this failure.

Health Care Utilization

Competition between physicians is not promoted by admission restrictions or restrictions on the freedom of establishment or other restraints but rather by publishing cost-benefit information. If admission restrictions would be removed the competition process between physicians may reduce the income level of this professional guild (Zweifel (2001)). But overall the health care market is characterized by imperfect market structures and rather SHI-controlled structures which determine the physicians' incomes and the attribution of costs (Leu (1987)). Therefore, it is unclear how the effects would be if admission restrictions would be reduced. In the future, for an adequate, good and at the same time affordable pharmaceutical therapy it will be essential that physicians find a balance between prescribing well tried or even generics and innovative pharmaceuticals.

The relationship between health care utilization and ageing depends on the reasons of decreasing death rates. If mortality falls because people are living healthier or because of more effective preventive measures, forecasts that do not take into account these causes will overestimate future health care expenditures. But if the death rates decrease only due to ever more complex technological or pharmaceutical innovations, the rising costs of such interventions will tend to annul the fact that fewer persons are in the last year of their life (Fuchs (1984)).

Use of Learning Effects

Hospitals invest in measuring their outcomes in order to document the cost-benefit ratio of their performances. According to the learning curve hypothesis of Ebbinghaus (1885) the outcome improves with repetition. Luft, Bunker, and Enthoven (1979) showed that the mortality rate decreased if operation teams undertake many surgical operations. Hence, it may be advantageous if hospitals merge and specialize in specific fields.

Care Vouchers

It is imaginable that within the SHI the title for care in old-age is received by offering care vouchers (Eisen (2006)). As the insurance carrier of the compulsory long term care insurance is combined with the SHI the benefit in kind vouchers can be issued by the selfsame. These care voucher could be acquired by caring for family members, relatives or other persons and could guarantee that oneself receive care in old age or if required. This would reduce the behaviourial modification due to being insured where usually prevention incentives are reduced. The specific implementation of the care voucher should be in such a manner that incentives are not inducing moral hazard and increasing total demand by offering benefits in kind. The idea behind this is that justice of a system is not defined by what you can take out but by what you give into it.

Valuation of Health Care Services

Regulative measures in the health care market could be founded on the evaluation of present value of these public expenditures as well as a cost analysis. Even if HCE are rising relative to GDP, the question comes up whether or not a resource reallocation from one sector to another is required. For instance, is it really necessary to subsidize kerosene which offers opportunities to fly around the world for a bargain price and simultaneously polluting the environment? How large should be the relation of public HCE to defence or traffic expenditures? Or should this money not put into HCE. For instance, since the last three decades the motor insurance rate increased by 20.8 percent but nobody would talk about a cost explosion in this area (German Insurance Association (2006)).

To evaluate the cost-benefit analysis, the expenditure structure should reflect to some extent individual preferences which could be captured within hypothetical scenarios applied in the stated preference technique. This technique is flexible and often used to capture preferences concerning policy reform relevant attributes. Alternatively, if data of real choices are given, the revealed preference technique can be applied to measure preferences of a representative sample by using observations on actual choices made by people (Earnhart (2001); Hicks (2002)). A main problem remains, namely, that preferences do not indicate the real demand structures within the prevailing health insurance market.

Value of Pharmaceutical Innovations

In the United States, the generic sector is dominated by unbranded compounds. Further, the total share of generics of 58 percent in unit volume is confronted with only 18 percent of sales share, pointing to the relative low prices of generics. Thus, in unit volume the total generic share covers 58 percent but in dollar terms the share of sales represents only 18 percent indicating that the average price of generics is rather low. In Germany, the total share of generics of 61 percent in units comprises only 34 percent of sales, showing relatively higher generic prices. But the relative higher prices of generics in Germany are due to the reference price limits on reimbursement (Danzon and Furukawa (2003)). This suggests that reference price limits on reimbursement are overvalued and should be marked down as producer of generics are only confronted with the production and distribution costs of generics without having to invest in risky, time-consuming, and capital intensive R&D.

Some also argue whether R&D expenditures are too high? But R&D has always been expensive. In the past it was mostly paid without restrictions. Nowadays it is scrutinised. Therefore, the question is how much R&D is required and how much society can afford. Therefore society, government, public health care insurance and the corresponding specialists have to specify the scope of benefits to answer this question. E.g. more cost-benefit analyses concerning new technologies and innovative pharmaceuticals are necessary.

Patent Law and Innovation Incentives

R&D is essential to enhance innovations, especially research and development concerning diseases that cause relative high damage to national economies due e.g. to unemployability. Therefore, curing chronical diseases is not only interesting for the pharmaceutical industry because of stable high rates of return but also for a country or rather social health care insurance itself. An evaluation of economic gains due to preventive measures should also be carried out. As patent rights are one possibility to achieve monopoly prices as well to increase costs of competitors and thus to secure the patentees' protection, they are supposed to increase innovation incentives.

Results from consistent refinement and R&D insights could be used to sustain patient oriented clinical research. Interdisciplinary centres for clinical research could modulate regional promotion of medical faculties. Additional, reviewing and publishing strategic approaches to the development of an innovating corporate culture could increase organizational knowledge of innovation creating processes.

In the recent past the discussion concerning patent rights mainly attracted attention because of two reasons. One reason covers the aspect of the infringement of a patent due to imitation, for instance by China. The other reason, substantially initiated by patent protection for software, points out the potential innovation inhibiting effect of current embodiment of the Patent Act. Between 1990 and 2000 the average yearly growth of patent application was 7.4 percent whereas the average growth of R&D expenditures was only 3.4 percent. This shows that the growth of patent applications was twice as much as the R&D expenditures. According to Advisory Council of the Federal Ministry of Economy and Technology ('Wissenschaftlicher Beirat beim Bundesministerium für Wirtschaft und Technologie' (2007)) this does not indicate an increased productivity but a change in behaviour of the patentees. Patentees start to build up patent portfolios in order to be able to sequentially develop innovations upon previous patented innovations. In this context patent protection could inhibit innovations by others. To avoid this development a Patent Act reform could be necessary.

More Saving - Incentives for Private Old-Age Provisions

It would be reasonable to save more in the younger years in order to be able to spend more or rather secure a certain life and health standard. These kind of arguments have been often discussed in the literature and is especially necessary for the currently younger. This is not tantamount to place emphasis only on alternative public financing schemes such as capital founded systems instead of pay-as-you-go systems. This argument stresses the fact that the currently younger cohorts have to look ahead to secure a certain level of provision in old-age phases. It seems correct that an increasing population of 65+ will spend more in old-age on health and long-term care. Therefore, tax relief may put the right incentives to save for old-ages. There exists, however, a lot of instruments to realize this goal, not only life policies or annuities.

Working Longer - Prolongation of the Labour Force Participation

To prolong the labour force participation one possibility is work longer. Therefore, a gradual increase in the age of retirement from the legally 65 years will start in 2012 and will reach the final age of retirement of 67 years in 2029 (Bundesministerium für Arbeit und Soziales (BMAS) (2006)). If number of years employed is 45 it will still be possible to retire with 65 years. The reform of the age of retirement was insofar necessary as the further life expectancy at age 65 has risen appreciable since 1975. But this change has not been accompanied by any increase in paid work of older men, and only a small increase for women (Fuchs (1998)). Increasing the age of retirement secures that enough money is saved in order to meet the demands in the old-age.

Increasing Fertility

Unfortunately, the German government missed the opportunity to create an adequate appealing child care infrastructure. Considering the current development there are too few child care places and this maybe is one reason that the actual debate calls for appropriate and flexible child care arrangements for at least one third of the babies and toddlers up to age of three years.

Current reform plans discuss that until 2013 one third of the parents should become entitled to obtain a child care place for their children. It seems that to give only financial incentives as e.g. children benefits was a rather onesided attempt to increase fertility. Another question is whether the traditional concept of family meets the actual development and changes of the last decades. In fact, an important aspect is to what extent child care can take place so that women can actually meet the demands of employment.

Considering the Demand of Elderly

The economic power of the elderly should not be neglected. More and more in marketing the elderly are discovered as new powerful target groups whose demand has to be met. Recently, industrial sectors such as the automobile branch detected the increased and different consumption structure of those population shares who are growing since the last decades. This 'senior part' of society often has large spending power and it is not uncommonly that the elderly have considerable financial resources. Given this fact, the insurers should develop and offer corresponding insurance contracts which satisfy the needs of the elderly.

Social Consensus Concerning Health Care Services

Finally, and this may the most difficult task of all, societies need to reach a social consensus concerning the extent of an appropriate level of the health care services for all age cohorts. For many goods and services the prevailing opinion is 'let the market decide'. According to standard economic theory the free choice of knowledgeable buyers paying with their own money for services provided by competitive suppliers should result in a socially efficient allocation of resources. Clearly, in imperfect markets such as the health care market the free interplay of market participants will not necessarily result in a socially efficient and 'fair' solution. However, much could be avoided to some extent through a redistribution of income without direct substitution. If society asks for a comprehensive health care system offering a broad range of health care services then HCE are more likely to increase. But if the goal is to achieve a low-cost health care system consequently the extent of health care service must be restricted. Therefore, the aim of public health care system should be clearly defined within a social consensus. As we all know that we are getting older we should make arrangements for this period of life and should not be surprised if we really are old.

Chapter 6

Deutschsprachige Zusammenfassung

Als eines der drängendsten Probleme für den modernen Wohlfahrtsstaat wird die Finanzierung seiner Kosten gesehen. Nichts liegt näher als die immer wieder geäußerte Befürchtung, dass die zahlenmäßige Zunahme der Älteren an der Bevölkerung, gekoppelt mit der individuellen Ausgabensteigerung mit dem Alter, die Gesundheitsausgaben unkontrolliert explodieren lässt (Steinmann und Telser (2005)). Innovationen im medizinischen Bereich sind für den größten Teil des Ausgabenwachstums verantwortlich. Daher enthält der Themenbereich Alterung, pharmazeutische Innovationen und Gesundheitsausgaben erheblichen politischen Zündstoff.
Um auf diese höchst brisanten Themenbereiche einzugehen, behandele ich in meiner Dissertation unterschiedliche Aspekte des Pharmamarktes, der Forschungs- und Entwicklungsanstrengungen der Pharma-Industrie auf die älter werdende Bevölkerung und die Entwicklung der Gesundheits- und Arzneimittelausgaben.
Das Forschungsthema lautet "Health Care Expenditures, Innovation, and Demographic Change". Meine Dissertation beruht im Wesentlichen auf den Ergebnissen der empirischen Forschung hinsichtlich der Gesundheitsausgaben bzw. der Arzneimittelausgaben und des Einflusses des Demographischen Wandels. Weiterhin untersuche ich den Einfluss von pharmazeutischen Innovationen auf diese Determinanten.

Preisregulierung im Pharmamarkt

Am Anfang der Forschungsanstrengungen haben wir in Eisen und Ilgin (2007) zunächst Regulationsmöglichkeiten des Pharmamarktes in den Vordergrund gestellt, um effektive Preisregulierungsmechanismen zu identifizieren. Daher liefert dieser erste Aufsatz ein detailiertes Bild der verschiedenen nationalen Preisregulierungsansätze.

Berücksichtigt man den zunehmenden politischen Druck steigender Gesundheitsausgaben, so stellt man fest, dass die Preisregulierung im pharmazeutischen Markt sich einer immer breiteren Anwendung erfreut. Diese Entwicklung der staatlichen Eingriffe wirft die Frage auf, inwiefern die Regulierung des Pharmamarktes ein geeignetes Mittel ist, um die steigenden Gesundheitsausgaben in den Griff zu bekommen. Je nach dem, welche Interessengruppe man vertritt, kann die Antwort unterschiedlich ausfallen. Tatsache ist, dass die meisten Staaten mit steigenden Gesundheitsausgaben konfrontiert sind und werden. Um die verschiedenen nationalen Preisregulierungsstrategien evaluieren zu können, müssen die zahlreichen Ansätze zunächst einmal dargestellt, bewertet und verglichen werden.

In der Literatur wird des Öfteren argumentiert, dass Regierungen versuchen sollten, die Preisobergrenzen für Arzneimittel möglichst niedrig anzusetzen. Berücksichtigt man allerdings, dass zu niedrig angesetzte Preisobergrenzen für Arzneimittel auch die Forschungs- und Entwicklungsanreize für die Pharma-Industrie reduzieren können, wird klar, dass solche Grenzen wohlüberlegt gewählt werden müssen.

Das Ziel dieses Aufsatzes ist es, die Effektivität ausgewählter Regulierungsmaßnahmen, die entweder die Angebots- oder die Nachfrageseite beeinflussen sollen, zu evaluieren. In Anbetracht der Globalisierung der Pharma-Industrie stellen internationale Evaluierungen einen wesentlichen Aspekt innerhalb der politischen und unternehmerischen Entscheidungsfindung dar. Nichtsdestotrotz haben internationale Evaluierungen wegen fehlender und inkonsistenter Daten keine Anwendung gefunden.

Aufgrund ungenügender, vergleichbarer Daten erfolgt in diesem Kapitel ein komparativer Überblick der verschiedenen existenten nationalen Preisregulierungen. Hierbei werden Patent-Regulierung und Parallelimporte auf der Angebotsseite und Arzneimittelbudgets, Generika und Festbeträge für Arzneimittel auf der Nachfrageseite der Preisregulierungsverfahren dargestellt und diskutiert.

Im Rahmen eines statischen zwei Klassen-Produktmodells wird der Einfluss von Festbeträgen untersucht. Unter Verwendung eines sequentiellen Preisfestlegungsprozesses kann mit Hilfe dieses Modells gezeigt werden, dass Festbeträge für Arzneimittel, die innerhalb der Stufe 1[1] klassifiziert werden und für die Preise in Höhe der Grenzkosten gelten, die Wohlfahrt

[1] Festbetragsregelungen finden im deutschen Gesundheitssystem und in den meisten Medicare Programmen der USA ihre Anwendung. In der Regel werden die Arzneimittel in drei Stufen in Gruppen zusammen gefasst. In der ersten Stufe werden generisch äquivalente Produkte und Arzneimittel, deren Patentschutz abgelaufen ist, zu einer Gruppe zusammengefasst. In der zweiten Stufe werden Gruppen für diejenigen Arzneimitteln gebildet,

erhöht werden kann. Festpreise in Höhe der Grenzkosten erhöhen die Wohlfahrt, ohne dass gesetzlichen Krankenkassen oder Generikahersteller als Trittbrettfahrer im Hinblick auf die versunkenen F&E-Kosten der forschenden Pharmaunternehmen agieren. Die in Stufe 1 zusammengefassten Arzneimittel haben ihren Patentschutz bereits verloren, d.h. die forschenden Pharmaunternehmen hatten während der Dauer des Patentschutzes die Möglichkeit, Monopolpreise zu erzielen und dadurch ihre F&E-Kosten zu amortisieren.

Um einen umfassenden Überblick bezüglich der anderen Preisregulierungsmechanismen zu geben, erfolgt eine Evaluierung der Interaktionen. In der Vergangenheit wurden zuviele Preisregulierungsmaßnahmen angewendet, die entweder nur an der Angebots- oder an der Nachfrageseite ansetzen. Allerdings ist von Preisregulierungsmaßnahmen, die nur einseitig wirken, nicht zu erwarten, dass sie die steigende Kostenentwicklung stoppen können. Ohne simultane Anwendung von Anreizen zur Ausgabenbegrenzung auf der Nachfrageseite und Volumina-Kontrollen auf der Angebotsseite, werden die Arzneimittelausgaben wohl kaum effektiv reduziert werden können.

Gesundheitsausgaben, Alterung und Pharmazeutische Innovation

In diesem Kapitel steht die Einflussrichtung des Demographischen Wandels und die des pharmazeutischen Fortschritts auf die Gesundheitsausgaben und hier insbesondere Arzneimittelausgaben im Vordergrund.

Betrachtet man bivariate Studien der ersten Generation, welche sich auf die Determinanten steigender Gesundheitsausgaben konzentrierten, deuteten diese auf den positiven Einfluss eines steigenden Bruttoinlandsprodukt (BIP) hin (Newhouse (1977)). Der Zusammenhang des BIP auf steigende Gesundheitsausgaben wurde zahlreich bestätigt u.a. durch Leu (1986), OECD (1987), Gerdtham, Sögaard, Andersson und Jönsson (1992) sowie Gerdtham, Sögaard, Jönsson und Andersson (1992).

Die Studien der zweiten Generation sind multivariate Ansätze. Hierbei deuten die Ergebnisse auf weitere Determinanten hin, welche die Gesundheitsausgaben erhöhen. Beispielsweise wird der Tabakkonsum, der Krankenversicherungsumfang oder die Anzahl der praktizierenden Ärtze identifiziert (Gerdtham, Jönsson, MacFarlan und Oxley (1998)). Später wird der technische

deren Wirkstoffe pharmakologisch, insbesondere chemisch, und dabei gleichzeitig auch hinsichtlich ihrer therapeutischen Wirkung vergleichbar sind. In der dritten Stufe werden all die Arzneimittel zusammengefasst, die hinsichtlich ihrer therapeutischen Wirkung vergleichbar sind. Für die jeweiligen Gruppen wird dann ein Festbetrag bzw. ein Höchstbetrag für die Erstattung von Arzneimittelpreisen durch die gesetzliche Krankenkasse bestimmt.

Fortschritt als eine der treibenden Kräfte für die steigenden Gesundheitsausgaben bestimmt (Newhouse (1992)).
Grundsätzlich könnte man erwarten, dass pharmazeutischen Innovationen "produziert" werden, wenn sich dadurch der Gewinn erhöhen lässt oder die Kosten senken lassen. Ein anderer Ansatz wäre es in Erfahrung zu bringen, durch welche Faktoren und in welche Richtung der pharmazeutische Fortschritt getrieben wird. In der Pharma-Industrie werden überwiegend neue Produkte, neue Wirkstoffe und damit Produktinnovationen hervorgebracht.
Oftmals wird in der Literatur argumentiert, dass Wettbewerb die Pharmaunternehmen zu einer immer rasanteren Entwicklung neuer Produkte zwingt. Dieser Wettbewerb führt schließlich bei Pharmaunternehmen zu einer Allokation von Ressourcen in die Marktsegmente mit hoher Gewinnerwartung. Zu beobachten ist diese Entwicklung in dem Bereich der chronischen Krankheit Diabetes. Es ist anzunehmen, dass sich die Forschungs- und Entwicklungsschwerpunkte an eher kurzfristigen Verwertungsinteressen mit langfristigen Gewinneinnahmen orientieren.
In diesem Kapitel geht es u.a. um die Frage, ob die Gesundheitsausgaben, genauer gesagt die darin enthaltenen Pharmaausgaben (Ausgaben für pharmazeutische Produkte) mit zunehmendem Lebensalter steigen. Man könnte auch danach fragen, ob die Zahlungsbereitschaft für Gesundheitsdienstleistungen und damit auch für Arzneimittel im Alter zunimmt. In diesem Fall würden sich der Demographische Wandel und die pharmazeutischen Innovationen als verstärkende Faktoren verhalten und damit eine langfristige Gesundheitsausgabensteigerung implizieren.
Für diese Art der sich verstärkenden Faktoren sprechen drei Aspekte: (1.) Der allgemeine Gesundheitszustand älterer Menschen ist im Durchschnitt schlechter als bei vergleichsweise jüngeren Menschen; (2.) das Sisyphus-Syndrom (Zweifel und Ferrari (1992)) und (3.) die Multimorbiditäts-Hypothese (Krämer (1996)).
Das Sisyphus-Syndrom beschreibt den Zusammenhang, dass medizinisch-technischer Fortschritt die Lebenserwartung verlängert und dadurch die Zahl derjenigen erhöht wird, die das Gesundheitswesen überdurchschnittlich beanspruchen. Aufgrund der erhöhten Anzahl von höher Betagten steigt auch ihr politisches Gewicht, so dass diese Gruppe der Alten in der Lage ist, politisch Druck auszuüben und im Gesundheitswesen immer mehr Wert auf Finanzierung weiterer kostspieliger medizinischer Innovationen gelegt wird. Diese werden durch

Steuergelder finanziert. Die Folge ist, dass die Erfolge der Medizin zu einer zunehmenden Belastung von Wirtschaft und Gesellschaft führen werden.

Dagegen beschreibt die Multimorbiditäts-Hypothese folgenden Zusammenhang: Ohne medizinisch-technischen Fortschritt wäre die Bevölkerung im Hinblick auf ihre selektive Mortalität heterogen und nur die "Fittesten" würden überleben. Wenn jetzt aber die Mortalitätsrate aufgrund des medizinisch-technischen Fortschritts sinkt, dann werden mehr alte und kranke Menschen überleben. Da aber das erfolgreiche Bekämpfen der ersten Krankheit (z.B. Herzkreislaufkrankheiten) die Menschen nicht gesünder machen wird, sondern nur die nächste zu behandelnde Krankheit, z.B. Krebs, einläutet, müssen die Kosten sich durch dieses Zusammenspiel von Alter und pharmazeutischen Innovationen gegenseitig verstärken und die Gesundheitsausgaben letztendlich steigen.

Wenn man allerdings annimmt, dass sich der Demographische Wandel und die pharmazeutische Innovationen als gegenseitig dämpfende Faktoren im Hinblick auf die Gesundheitsausgaben verhalten, so könnte man mit der "Nähe zum Tod" argumentieren bzw. damit, dass die meisten Gesundheitsausgaben im letzten Jahr vor dem Tod getätigt werden (Fuchs (1984)). Die in Querschnittsdaten beobachtbare Differenz in den Gesundheitsausgaben zwischen älteren und jüngeren Versicherten wäre folglich nicht allein bzw. nicht primär mit dem Lebensalter erklärbar, sondern mit der unterschiedlichen Nähe zum Tod. In höheren Altersgruppen befindet sich ein größerer Anteil Versicherten im letzten Lebensjahr - und im letzten Lebensjahr wird in Rahmen eines vergeblichen Versuchs, den Tod noch abzuwenden - überproportional mehr für Behandlung aufgewendet als in den Jahren davor. Steigt nun durch technischen Fortschritt oder gesündere Lebensweise die Lebenserwartung, so sinkt die Sterbeziffer, und in jeder Altersgruppe befinden sich damit weniger Personen in ihrem letzten Lebensjahr. Trifft diese These zu, so müssten sich die altersspezifischen Behandlungskosten in betroffenen Altersgruppen über die Zeit verringern.

Die These der "Nähe zum Tod" ist tatsächlich mehrfach bestätigt worden, u.a. durch Lubitz, Beebe und Baker (1995) . Die Autoren konnten anhand von Daten der Medicare-Verwaltung der USA zeigen, dass 27-30% der Medicare Aufwendungen eines Jahres an Personen erbracht wurden, die ein Jahr später nicht mehr am Leben waren. Die Pro-Kopf-Ausgaben waren siebenmal so hoch wie für gleichaltrige, die nicht in ihrem letzten Lebensjahr standen. Zweifel, Felder und Meier (1996) fanden für eine Schweizer Stichprobe Belege für ein

Verhältnis von 5,3 zu 1 und Busse, Krauth und Schwartz (2002) fanden für eine Stichprobe einer Ersatzkrankenkasse 4 bis 30mal so hohe Ausgaben, wie bei gleichaltrigen Überlebenden. Betrachtet man nun die Ausgaben für verschreibungspflichtige Arzneimittel, so stellt man fest, dass diese seit Mitte der 1990er Jahre schneller gestiegen sind als jede andere wichtige Komponente der Gesundheitsausgaben. Daher ist ein internationaler Vergleich der Ursachen von großem Interesse (DiMasi, Hansen und Grabowski (2003)). Hierzu haben wir die Daten von sieben Ländern, nämlich Australien, Deutschland, Finnland, Frankreich, Kanada, Japan und USA, über einen Zeitraum von 11 Jahren (1991-2001) herangezogen. Die OECD Health Data 2005 bilden die Datengrundlage für die durchgeführte Panelanalyse. Die Forschungsaktivität der Pharmaunternehmen wird durch Daten des Jahresberichtes 2005 des Europäischen Patentamtes instrumentalisiert.

Zwei alternative Schätzmethoden wurden hierbei implementiert: Zum einen der Fixed-Effects-Schätzer und zum anderen die Generalised Method of Moments (GMM) Methode. Dahinter steht die Idee, immer angemessenere Schätzer zu verwenden, um die jeweiligen Verbesserungen der unterschiedlichen Methoden deutlich zu machen. Bei dem Fixed-Effects-Ansatz wird unterstellt, dass die Koeffizient zwar unbekannt, aber fix sind. Folglich werden die zeitinvarianten, länderspezifischen Effekte erfasst. Um dynamische Effekte zu erfassen, wurde der GMM-Schätzer (mit ersten Differenzen) angewendet.

Die empirische Auswertung belegt, dass die zunehmende Häufigkeit der Arztkonsultation die Arzneimittelausgaben reduzieren. Hier gibt es demzufolge keine Anzeichen für ein Moral Hazard Verhalten der Ärzte beim Verschreiben von Arzneimitteln. Es ist anzunehmen, dass eher Kontroll- mit Folgeuntersuchung ohne Arzneimittelverschreibung erfolgen. Des Weiteren zeigen die Resultate, dass die Arzneimittelausgaben mit steigender (Rest-) Lebenserwartung und mit steigendem Bevölkerungsanteil der über 65jährigen (Nachfragekomponente) ebenfalls zunehmen. Auch steigen die Arzneimittelausgaben mit zunehmendem Produktionswert und steigender F&E Ausgaben der Pharma-Industrie (Angebotskomponente). Die empirische Analyse deckt diesbezüglich erste Strukturkomponenten der Arzneimittelausgaben auf, die sowohl angebots- als auch nachfrageinduzierte (altersbedingte) Kostensteigerungseffekte auslösen. Die zunehmenden F&E Ausgaben der Pharmaindustrie (Angebotskomponente) und die steigende Restlebenserwartung der über 65jährigen (Nachfragekomponente) führen andererseits auch zu einer Zunahme der pharmazeutischen Innovationen. Die Zunahme von pharmazeutischen Innovationen führen wiederum zu erhöhten Heilungschancen von Krankheiten, aber auch zum Steigen der Arzneimittelausgaben. Allerdings ist im Hinblick auf die Aggregation der Daten (Makrodaten) Vorsicht geboten, da diese zu Verzerrungen führen könnten. Schließlich sind es bei Analysen auf dem Mikrolevel nicht der demographische Wandel und das Steigen der Restlebenserwartung, die zur Steigerung der Gesundheitsausgaben führen, sondern die Nähe zum Tod (Zweifel (2001)). Weiterhin ist unklar, ob die Nähe zum Tod bei Arzneimittelausgaben mehr Varianz aufklärt als das Alter bzw. die Restlebenserwartung, und es ergibt sich das Problem, dass die Nähe zum Tod aufgrund der aktuellen Datenlage noch nicht analysierbar ist.

Der Zusammenhang zwischen pharmazeutischen Innovationen, Gesundheitsausgaben in Deutschland und Mortalität

Im vierten Kapitel wird mittels eines vektorautoregressiven Modells der Zusammenhang zwischen den öffentlichen Gesundheitsausgaben, den potentiell verlorenen Lebensjahre und der Wirkstoffzulassung durch das Bundesinstituts für Arzneimittel und Medizinprodukte in Deutschland untersucht. Bei dieser Analyse handelt es sich um eine multivariate Zeitreihenanalyse. Hierbei wird ein ökonometrisches Mehrgleichungsmodell mit drei Gleichungen geschätzt. In diesem Gleichungssystem werden alle drei interessierenden Variablen als Funktion der übrigen Variablen dargestellt. Die jeweilige Variable wird nur aus ihrem eigenen zeitlichen Verlauf sowie der zeitlichen Entwicklung der anderen endogenen Variablen heraus erklärt.

Die Gesundheitsausgabengleichung zeigt einen positiven Zusammenhang zwischen den potentiell verlorenen Lebensjahre und den öffentlichen Gesundheitsausgaben. Sinken die potentiell verlorenen Lebensjahre, dann sinken auch die öffentlichen Gesundheitsausgaben. Anders formuliert, steigen die potentiell verlorenen Lebensjahre eher kurzfristig betrachtet, so steigen die Gesundheitsausgaben. Folglich steigen die Gesundheitsausgaben in Deutschland mit steigenden verlorenen Lebensjahren und zunehmenden Wirkstoffzulassungen. Diese Effekte werden signifikant. Die Ergebnisse stehen im Einklang mit den vorangegangenen Überlegungen, dass der Staat höhere Ausgaben für Gesundheitsleistungen tätigen wird, wenn die potentiell verlorenen Lebensjahre zunehmen.

Es ist davon auszugehen, dass im Falle eines Steigens potentiell verlorener Lebensjahren, der politische Druck steigen wird. Die Regierung wird unter Zuhilfenahme öffentlicher Gesundheitsausgaben versuchen, der Erhöhung potentiell verlorener Lebensjahre entgegenzuwirken. Die Ergebnisse zeigen auch, dass langfristig getätigte Gesundheitsausgaben einen positiven Einfluss auf das gegenwärtige Ausgabenniveau haben. Folglich schlägt sich vergangenes hohes Ausgabenniveau auch in einem hohem gegenwärtigen Ausgabenniveau nieder.

In der Gleichung der potentiell verlorenen Lebensjahre werden nur die kurzfristigen potentiell verlorenen Lebensjahre vergangener Jahre signifikant. Sind in der Vergangenheit die potentiell verlorenen Lebensjahre gesunken, so sinkt auch gegenwärtig die Anzahl der potentiell verlorenen Lebensjahre.

Ergebnisse der Wirkstoffzulassungsgleichung zeigen, dass mit kurzfristig steigenden öffentlichen Gesundheitsausgaben auch die Wirkstoffzulassungen steigen. Folglich kommt es zu einem Angebotseffekt durch Pharmaunternehmen sobald Gesundheitsausgaben zunehmen. Allerdings zeigen die Ergebnisse auch, dass die Wirkstoffzulassungen langfristig mit steigenden Gesundheitsausgaben sinken. Dieser Zusammenhang lässt sich mittels Kosteneindämmungsversuchen der deutschen Regierung erklären. Die potentiell verlorenen Lebensjahre beeinflussen die Wirkstoffzulassung sowohl kurz- als auch langfristig signifikant. Überraschenderweise sinken die Wirkstoffzulassungen kurzfristig mit einer Zunahme der potentiell verlorenen Lebensjahre. Dies kann allerdings an der Datengrundlage liegen. Übereinstimmend mit vorangegangen Überlegungen steigen die Wirkstoffzulassung mit einer Zunahme der potentiell verlorenen Lebensjahre. Folglich werden Wirkstoffzulassungen für Arzneimittel steigen, d.h. es wird mehr geforscht, wenn die Menschen früher sterben oder mehr Geld ins Gesundheitswesen fließt und somit der Markt attraktiver für potentielle Innovationen wird.

Es wurde auch angenommen, dass die potentiell verlorenen Jahre sinken, wenn mehr Geld ins Gesundheitswesen investiert wird. Das Gleiche gilt, wenn mehr Wirkstoffe zugelassen werden und somit mehr Krankheiten behandelbar werden. Allerdings wird dieser Zusammenhang nicht signifikant. Dies kann mehrere Gründe haben. Es könnte an der Datengrundlage oder auch an der tendenziell weit gehaltenen Definition der Variable potentiell verlorene Lebensjahr liegen, die zum einen nur die potentiell verlorenen Lebensjahre bis zum Alter von 70 Jahren erfasst und zum anderen nicht nur durch pharmazeutische Innovationen sondern auch medizinisch-technischen Innovationen, wie beispielsweise im Bereich der Operationsmethoden, beeinflusst wird.

Übersetzt man diese Ergebnisse in konkrete, ökonomische Outputs, so kann die Verlängerung der aktiven Lebenszeit auch eine Erhöhung der Arbeitsproduktivität zur Folge haben. Ein größeres Arbeitskräftepotential führt nicht nur zu einer Erweiterung des Pools potentieller Arbeitskräfte und dadurch zu einer möglichen Verbesserung der Arbeitsproduktivität, sondern auch dazu, dass Arbeitskosten gesenkt werden.

Zusammenfassung - Einige Schlussfolgerungen und politische Implikationen

In Kapitel 5 werden die eigenen und weitere internationale und nationale Forschungsergebnisse zusammengefasst. Basierend auf diesen werden politische Implikationen abgeleitet.

Hierfür wird an unterschiedlichen Ebenen angesetzt und diverse Aspekte werden angesprochen. Dazu gehört ein verbessertes Informationsmanagement, die Regulierungsmöglichkeiten der Inanspruchnahme von Gesundheitsleistungen, die Nutzbarmachung von Lerneffekten und die Ausgabe von Pflegegutscheinen. Des Weiteren spielen die Wertschätzung von Gesundheitsdienstleistungen und pharmazeutischer Innovation, der Einfluss des Patentgesetzes und die Schaffung von Innovationsanreizen eine nicht unbedeutende Rolle. Anreize zu vermehrtem Sparen und einer Verlängerung der Arbeitszeit, die Erhöhung der Fertilität oder die Berücksichtigung der Nachfragstrukturen der Älteren sind weitere Einflussfaktoren. Aber der wahrscheinlich schwierigste Schritt in Hinblick auf den Umfang der Gesundheitsdienstleistungen, ist das Finden eines sozialen Konsens.

In Anbetracht der Tatsache, dass wir alle immer älter werden, sollte jeder diesbezüglich Vorkehrung treffen, um dann nicht doch vom Alter überrascht zu werden. Oder um den berühmten Dichterfürst Johann Wolfgang von Goethe mit dem Gedicht "Das Alter" zu zitieren:

> Das Alter ist ein höflich Mann:
> Einmal übers andre klopft er an;
> Aber nun sagt niemand: Herein!
> Und vor der Türe will er nicht sein.
> Da klinkt er auf, tritt ein so schnell,
> Und nun heißt's, er sei ein grober Gesell.

Bibliography

AHN, S., AND P. SCHMIDT (1995): "Efficient estimation of models for dynamic panel data," *Journal of Econometrics*, 68, 5–27.

ARELLANO, M., AND S. BOND (1991): "Some Tests of Specification for Panel Data: Monte Carlo Evidence and an Application to Employment Equations," *Review of Economic Studies*, 58, 277–297.

AVORN, J., I. CHOODNOVSKIY, T. MYLAUGHLIN, D. ROSS-DEGNAN, AND J. SOURMERAL (1991): "Effects of Medicaid drug-payment limits on admission to hospitals and nursing homes," *New England Journal of Medicine*, 325, 1072–1077.

BALESTRA, P. (1995): "Introduction to Linear Models for Panel Data," in *The Econometrics of Panel Data: Handbook of the Theory with Appilications*, ed. by L. Mátyás, and P. Sevestre, pp. 25–33. Kluwer Academic Publisher.

BARZEL, Y. (1968): "Optimal Timing of Innovation," *The Review of Economics and Statistics*, 50(3), 348–355.

BAUMOL, W. J. (1967): "Macroeconomics of Unbalanced Growth: The Anatomy of Urban Crisis," *American Economic Review*, 57(3), 415–426.

BGA (2004): "Glossar: Festbeträge," Glossar, Gemeinsamer Bundesausschuss, Siegburg, http://www.g-ba.de/cms/front_content.php?idcat=32(14.11.2004).

BLOOM, D. (2001): "The Effects of Health on Economic Growth: Theory and Evidence," Nber working paper series no.8587, NBER, Cambridge.

BLUNDELL, R., AND S. BOND (1998): "Initial conditions and moment restrictions in dynamic panel data models," *Journal of Econometrics*, 87, 115–143.

BLUNDELL, R., S. BOND, AND F. WINDMEIJER (2000): "Estimation in Dynamic Panel Data Models: Improving on the Performance of the Standard GMM Estimators," Working paper, University College London and Institute of Fiscal Studies.

BREYER, F. (2000): "Zukunftperspektiven der Gesundheitssicherung," *Zeitschrift für Wirtschafts- und Sozialwissenschaften - Die Zukunft des Sozialstaats*, Beiheft 8, 167–199.

BREYER, F., AND S. FELDER (2004): "Life Expectancy and Health Care Expenditures: A New Calculation for Germany Using the Costs of Dying," Discussion paper no. 452, DIW, Berlin.

BREYER, F., AND V. ULRICH (2000): "Gesundheitsausgaben, Alter und medizinischer Fortschritt: Eine Regressionsanalyse," *Jahrbücher für Nationalökonomie und Statistik*, 220(1), 1–17.

BREYER, F., P. S. ZWEIFEL, AND M. KIFMANN (2005): *Gesundheitökonomie*. Springer, Berlin, 5th edn.

BUNDESMINISTERIUM FÜR ARBEIT UND SOZIALES (BMAS) (2006): "Erhöhung des Renteneintrittsalters von 65 auf 67 Jahre," Discussion paper, BMAS, Berlin, http://www.bmas.bund.de/BMAS/Navigation/Presse/nachrichten,did=110752.html (18.05.2007).

BUNDESMINISTERIUM FÜR GESUNDHEIT (2007): "Kennzahlen und Faustformeln," Discussion paper, Bundesministerium für Gesundheit, Berlin, http://www.bmg.bund.de/cln_041/nn_601096/SharedDocs/Download/DE/Datenbanken-Statistiken/Statistiken-Gesundheit/Gesetzliche-Krankenversicherung/Kennzahlen-und-Faustformeln/Kennzahlen-und-Faustformeln,templateId=raw,property=publication File.pdf/Kenn zahlen-und-Faustformeln.pdf (24.04.2007).

BUSSE, R., C. KRAUTH, AND F. W. SCHWARTZ (2002): "Use of acute hospital beds does not increase as the population ages: Results for a seven year cohort study in Germany," *Journal of Epidemiology and Community Health*, 56, 289–293.

CAMBOIS, E., AND J.-M. ROBINE (1996): "An International Comparison of Trends in Disability-Free Life Expectancy," in *Long-Term Care: Economic Issues and Policy Solutions*, ed. by R. Eisen, and F. Sloan, pp. 11–23. Kluwer Academic Publishers.

CAVES, R. E., M. D. WHINSTON, AND M. A. HURWITZ (1991): "Patent Expiration, Entry, and Competition in the U.S. Pharmaceutical Industry," *Brooking Papers on Economic Activity. Microeconomics*, 1991, 1–66.

CUTLER, DAVID, M., AND M. MCCELLAN (2001): "Is Technological Change In Medicine Worth It," *Health Affairs*, 20(5), 11–29.

DANZON, PATRICIA, M. (1997a): *Pharmaceutical Price Regulation: National Policies and Global Interests*. The AEI Press, Washington, D.C.

DANZON, P. M. (1997b): "Price Discrimination for Pharmaceuticals: Welfare Effects in the US and the EU," *International Journal of the Economics of Business*, 4(3), 301–321.

DANZON, P. M., AND M. F. FURUKAWA (2003): "Prices and Availability of Pharmaceuticals: Evidence from Nine Countries," *Health Affairs*, Web Exclusive - 29 October 2003, 521–536.

DANZON, P. M., AND J. D. KETCHAM (2003): "Reference Pricing of Pharmaceuticals for Medicare: Evidence from Germany, the Netherlands and New Zealand," Working paper, NBER, Cambridge, http://www.nber.org/papers/w10007.

DIMASI, J., R. W. HANSEN, AND H. G. GRABOWSKI (2003): "The price of innovation: new estimates of drug development costs," *Journal of Health Economics*, 22, 151–185.

DINKEL, R. H. (1999): "Demographische Entwicklung und Gesundheitszustand," in *Gesundheit - unser höchstes Gut?*, ed. by H. Häfner, pp. 61–83. Springer.

EARNHART, D. (2001): "Combining Revealed and Stated Preference Methods to Value Environmental Amenities at Residential Locations," *Land Economics*, 77(1), 12–29.

EBBINGHAUS, H. (1885): *Über das Gedächtnis: Untersuchungen zur experimentellen Psychologie*. Wissenschaftliche Buchgesellschaft, Darmstadt.

EIFF, W. V., T. MASSARO, J. VOO, AND R. ZIEGENBEIN (2002): "Medical Saving Accounts: a core feature of Singapore's health care system," *European Journal of Health Economics*, 3, 188–195.

EISEN, R. (2006): "10 Years of Social Long-term Care Insurance in Germany - What We Wanted, what We Got, what We Expect," *Schweizerische Zeitschrift für Volkswirtschaft und Statistik*, Special Issue 2006, 29–35.

EISEN, R., AND Y. ILGIN (2007): "Pricing Policies for the Pharmaceutical Market - An International Perspective," in *Trade, Integration, and Institutional Reforms*, ed. by R. Eisen, A. Cafferata, E. Neder, and M. L. Recalde, pp. 203–222. Peter Lang.

ERBSLAND, M., W. RIED, AND V. ULRICH (1999): "Die Auswirkungen der Bevölkerungsstruktur auf Ausgaben und Beitragssatz der gesetzlichen Krankenversicherung," in *Entwicklung und Perspektiven der Sozialversicherung: Beiträge zum ZEW-Symposium: Ansätze zur Reform des Steuer- und Sozialversicherungssystems am 10. und 11. März 1997 in Mannheim*, ed. by E. Wille, pp. 173–197. Nomos Verlag.

EUROPEAN COUNCIL, P. (1998): "Council Decision of February (98/44/EC)," *Official Journal of the European Communities*, 44, 13–21.

EUROPEAN COMMISSION (2003a): "Commission Communication on Parallel Imports of Proprietary Medicinal Products for which Marketing Authorisations have already been granted," *Communication from the Commission of the European Communities*, COM/2003/0839 final, 1–17.

——— (2003b): "Parallel Trade," Glossary, European Commission, Brussel, http://europa.eu.int/comm/competition/general_info/p_en.html.

FELDER, S. (2006): "Lebenserwartung, medizinischer Fortschritt und Gesundheitsausgaben: Theorie und Empirie," *Perspektiven der Wirtschaftpolitik*, 7, 49–73.

FRANK, R. G. (2003): "Editorial: New estimates of drug development costs," *Journal of Health Economics*, 22, 325–330.

FREYTAG, C. (2001): *Parallelimporte nach EG- und WTO-Recht: Patente und Marken versus Handelsfreiheit*. Duncker und Humblot, Berlin.

FRIES, J. F. (1985): "The compression of morbidity," *World Health Forum*, 6, 47–51.

FUCHS, V. R. (1984): ""Though Much is Taken" – Reflections on Aging, Health, and Medical Care," Working paper, National Bureau of Economic Research, Cambridge, http://www.nber.org/papers/w1269.

——— (1998): "Provide, Provide: The Economics of Aging," Working paper, National Bureau of Economic Research, Cambridge, http://www.nber.org/papers/w6642.

GELJINS, A. C., AND N. ROSENBERG (1994): "The Dynamics of Technological Change in Medicine," *Health Affairs*, 13, 28–46.

GERDTHAM, U.-G., AND B. JÖNSSON (2000): "International Comparison of Health Expenditure: Theory, Data and Econometric Analysis," in *Handbook of Health Economics*, ed. by A. Culyer, and J. Newhous, pp. 11–53. Elsevier.

GERDTHAM, U.-G., B. JÖNSSON, M. MACFARLAN, AND H. OXLEY (1998): "A Pooled Cross-Section Analysis of the Health Expenditure of the OECD Countries," in *Health, The Medical Profession, and Regulation*, ed. by P. Zweifel. Kluwer Academic Publishers.

GERDTHAM, U.-G., F. SÖGAARD, F. ANDERSSON, AND B. JÖNSSON (1992): "Econometric Analysis of Health Expenditure: A Cross-sectional Study of the OECD Countries," *Journal of Health Economics*, 11, 63–84.

GERDTHAM, U.-G., F. SÖGAARD, B. JÖNSSON, AND F. ANDERSSON (1992): "A Pooled Cross-Section Analysis of the Health Expenditure of the OECD Countries," in *Health Economics Worldwide*, ed. by P. Zweifel, and H. Frech. Kluwer Academic Publishers.

GERMAN FEDERAL INSITUTE FOR DRUGS AND MEDICAL DEVICES (BFARM) (2006): "Processing Statistic of the BfArM 1986-2004," Discussion paper, Bundesministerium für Arzneimittel und Medizinprodukte (BfArM), Bonn.

GERMAN INSURANCE ASSOCIATION (2006): *Statistical Yearbook of German Insurance 2006*. German Insurance Association, Berlin.

GOATE, P., J. RHYS, AND F. GERNER (1999): "The Economic Consequences of the Choice of Regime of Exhaustion in the Area of Trademarks," Final report, Executive Summary of the Final Report for DG XV of the European Commission, London, http://europa.eu.int/comm/dg15/intprop/tmstudy.htm.

GODDEERIS, J. H. (1984): "Insurance and Incentives for Innovation in Medical Care," *Southern Economic Journal*, 51(2), 530–539.

GREENE, W. H. (2003): *Econometric Anaysis*. Prentice-Hall, London.

HALL, R. E., AND C. I. JONES (2004): "The Value of Life and the Rise in Health Spending," Working paper, NBER, Cambridge, http://www.nber.org/papers/w10737.

HAMILTON, J. D. (1994): *Time series Analysis*. Princeton University Press, Princeton, New Jersey.

HICKS, R. L. (2002): "A Comparision of Stated and Revealed Preference Methods for Environmental Management," Working paper, The College of William and Mary, Williamsburg.

HUJER, R., U. BLIEN, M. CALIENDO, AND C. ZEISS (2002): "Macroeconometric Evaluation of Active Labour Market Policies in Germany - A Dynamic Panel Approach Using Regional Data," Working Paper, J.W.Goethe-University, Frankfurt.

ILGIN, Y. (2007): "Pharmaceutical Innovations, German Health Care Expenditures, and Mortality," Working paper, Institute of European Health Policy and Social Law (INEGES), Frankfurt/M.

ILGIN, Y., AND R. EISEN (2007): "Health Care Expenditures, Ageing Population and Pharmaceutical Innovation," Working paper, Institute of European Health Policy and Social Law (INEGES), Frankfurt/M.

IMS HEALTH (2004): *Pricing and Reimbursement: Review 2003*. Cambridge Pharma Consultancy, Cambridge.

JASPER, J., AND R. TROSTMANN (2005): "Innovationseffekte von Patentrechtsreform und neuer Festbetragsregel," *List Forum für Wirtschafts- und Finanzpolitik*, 31(4), 319–340.

KANAVOS, P., J. COSTA-I FONT, S. MERKUR, AND M. GEMMILL (2003): "The Economic Impact of Pharmaceutical Parallel Trade: A Stakeholder Analysis. Key Study Findings," Working paper, The London School of Economics and Political Science, London, http://www.lse.ac.uk/collections/pressAndInformationOffice/newsAndEvents (10.10.2004).

KIVIET, J. (1995): "On bias, inconsistency, and efficiency of various estimators in dynamic panel data models," *Journal of Econometrics*, 68, 53–78.

KÖNIGBAUER, I. (2004): "The effect of parallel imports on the pharmaceutical price regulation," Working paper, University of Munich, Munich.

KRÄMER, W. (1996): "Hippocrates und Sisyphus - die moderne Medizin als Opfer ihres eigenen Erfolges," in *Rationierung im Gesundheitswesen*, ed. by H. Kirch, W. und Kliemt, pp. 389–393. Roderer Verlag.

LEU, R. E. (1986): "The Public-Private Mix and International Health Care Costs," in *Public and Private Health Services*, ed. by A. Culyer, and B. Jönsson. Basil Blackwell.

LEU, R. E. (1987): "Technologischer Wandel im Gesundheitswesen - Determinanten und Auswirkungen," in *Technologischer Wandel im Gesundheitswesen*, ed. by G. Gäfgen, and P. Oberender, pp. 9–33. Nomos Verlagsgesellschaft.

LICHTENBERG, F. R. (1998): "Pharmaceutical Innovation, Mortality Reduction, and Economic Growth," Working paper, NBER, Cambridge, http://www.nber.org/papers/w6569.

——— (2001): "Are the Benefits of Newer Drugs Worth their Costs? Evidence from the 1996 MEPS," *Health Affairs*, 20(5), 241–251.

LÜTKEPOHL, H. (1993): *Introduction to multiple time series analysis*. Springer, Berlin.

LU, Z. J., AND W. S. COMANOR (1998): "Strategic pricing of new pharmaceuticals," *The Review of Economics and Statistics*, 8(1), 108–118.

LUBITZ, J. D., J. BEEBE, AND C. BAKER (1995): "Longevity and Medicare Expenditures," *The New England Journal of Medicine*, 332(15), 999–1003.

LUCAS, R. E. (1976): "Econometric Policy Evaluation: A Critique," *Carnegie-Rochester Conference Series on Public Policy*, 1, 19–46.

LUFT, H., J. BUNKER, AND A. ENTHOVEN (1979): "Should operations be regionalized? The empirical relation between surgical volume and mortality," *New England Journal of Medicine*, 301, 1364–1369.

MRAZEK, M. F. (2002): "Comparative Approaches to Pharmaceutical Price Regulation in the European Union," *Croatian Medical Journal*, 43(4), 453–461.

NEWHOUSE, J. P. (1977): "Medical Care Expenditure: A Cross-National Survey," *Journal of Human Ressources*, 12, 115–125.

——— (1992): "Medical Care Costs: How Much Welfare Loss," *Journal of Economic Perspectives*, 6(3), 3–21.

NINK, K. (2005): *Price Development in the Pharmaceutical Market until 2005 - German Index*. Research Institute of general regional sickness funds (WIdO), Bonn.

OECD (1987): "Financing and Delivering Health Care: A Comparative Analysis of Seven OECD Countries," *OECD Social Policy*, 4.

——— (1995): *The Measurement of Scientific and Technological Activities. Proposed Guidelines for Collecting and Interpreting Technological Innovation Data. Oslo Manual*. OECD, 2nd edn.

——— (2005): *OECD Health Data 2005*. OECD Publishing, Paris.

——— (2006): *OECD Health Data 2006*. OECD Publishing, Paris.

OKUNADE, A., AND V. MURTHY (2002): "Technology as a 'major driver' of health care costs: a cointegration analysis of the Newhouse conjecture," *Journal of Health Economics*, 21(1), 147–159.

POSTLER, A. (2003): "Modellrechnung zur Beitragentwicklung in der Gesetzlichen Krankenversicherung: Auswirkungen von demographischen Wandel und medizinisch-technischen Fortschritt," Discussion paper no. 298, Universität Duisburg-Essen, Duisburg.

PROGNOS (1998): *Auswirkungen veränderter ökonomischer und rechtlicher Rahmenbedingungen auf die gesetztliche Rentenversicherung in Deutschland*. DRV-Schriften, Frankfurt/M.

SCHERER, F. M. (2000): "The Pharmaceutical Industry," in *Handbook of Health Economics*, ed. by A. Culyer, and J. Newhous, pp. 1297–1336. Elsevier.

——— (2001): "The Link between Gross Profitability and Pharmaceutical R&D Spending," *Health Affairs*, 20(5), 216–220.

SCHREYÖGG, J., AND R. BUSSE (2004): "Physician Drug Budget in Germany: Effects on Prescription Behaviour," Discussion paper, Department of Health Care Management, Berlin, http://www.dh.gov.uk/PublicationsAndStatistics/PressReleases/PressReleasesNotices/fs/en?CONTENT_ID=4093244&chk=3b4R7Y.

SCHWABE, U. (2006): "Arzneimittelverordnungen 2004 im Überblick," in *Arzneimittelverordnungsreport*, ed. by U. Schwabe, and D. Paffrath, pp. 3–36. Springer.

SMITH, S. R. (2002): "Multinational economic evaluations of pharmaceuticals," *The Lancet*, 360, 816.

STEINMANN, L., AND H. TELSER (2005): "Gesundheitskosten in der alternden Gesellschaft," Executive summary, Avenir Suisse, Zurich.

U.S. GENERAL ACCOUNTING OFFICE (GAO) (1994): "National Laboratories: Are Their R&D Activities Related to Commercial Product Development?," Report, GAO, Washington, DC, GAO/PEMD-95-2.

VERBRUGGE, L. M. (1984): "Longer Life but Worsening Health? Trends in Health and Mortality of Middle-Aged and Older Persons," *Millbank Memorial Found Quarterly*, 62, 475–519.

VFA (2004): *The Pharmaceutical Industry in Germany*. Verband Forschender Arzneimittelhersteller e.V., Berlin.

——— (2006): *The Pharmaceutical Industry in Germany*. German Association of Research-Based Pharmaceutical Companies, Berlin.

VON GOETHE, J. W. (2007): *Johann Wolfgang Goethe - Sämtlich Gedichte*. Insel Verlag, Frankfurt.

WEISBROD, B. A. (1991): "The Health Care Quadrilemma: An Essay on Technological Change, Insurance, Quality of Care, and Cost Containment," *Journal of Economic Literature*, 29(2), 523–552.

WIPO (2005): "Annual Statistics 1978-2004," Report, World Intellectual Property Organization (WIPO), Geneva, http://www.wipo.int/ipstats/en/statistics/patents/pdf/yearly_ report_2004.pdf.

WISSENSCHAFTLICHER BEITRAG DES BMWI (2007): "Patentschutz und Innovation," Gutachten, Bundesministerium für Wirtschaft und Technologie (BMWi), Berlin.

ZWEIFEL, P. (2000): "Eine Gesundheitspolitik für das 21. Jahrhundert: Zehn Reformvorschläge," *Perspektiven der Wirtschaftspolitik*, 2(1), 81–98.

——— (2001): "Alter, Gesundheit und Gesundheitsausgaben - eine neue Sicht," *G+G Wissenschaft (GGW)*, 1, 6–12.

ZWEIFEL, P., S. FELDER, AND M. MEIER (1996): "Demographische Alterung und Gesundheitskosten: Eine Fehlinterpretation," in *Alter und Gesundheit*, ed. by Oberender, pp. 29–46. Nomos Verlagsgesellschaft.

ZWEIFEL, P., AND M. FERRARI (1992): "Is there a Sisyphus Syndrom in Health Care?," in *Health Economics Worldwide - Developments in Health Economics and Public Policy Series*, ed. by P. Zweifel, and H. III. Ferch, vol. 1, pp. 311–330. Kluwer Academic.

ZWEIFEL, P., L. STEINMANN, AND P. EUGSTER (2005): "The Sisphus Syndrom in Health Revisted," *International Journal of Health Care Finance and Economics*, 5(2), 127–145.

Frankfurter Schriften zur Gesundheitspolitik
und zum Gesundheitsrecht
Schriftenreihe des Instituts für Europäische Gesundheitspolitik und Sozialrecht
an der Johann Wolfgang Goethe-Universität Frankfurt

Herausgegeben von Ingwer Ebsen und Roland Eisen

Band 1 Dominik Roters: Die gebotene Kontrolldichte bei der gerichtlichen Prüfung der Richtlinien des Bundesausschusses der Ärzte und Krankenkassen. 2003.

Band 2 Carsten Wendtland: Die Forschung mit menschlichen embryonalen Stammzellen als Gegenstand der Rechtsetzung. 2005.

Band 3 Johannes Pantel / Gisela Bockenheimer-Lucius / Ingwer Ebsen / Ruth Müller / Peter Hustedt / Alexander Diehm: Psychopharmakaversorgung im Altenpflegeheim. Eine interdisziplinäre Studie unter Berücksichtigung medizinischer, ethischer und juristischer Aspekte. 2006.

Band 4 Christel Köhler-Hohmann: Die Teilnahme der Ärzte- bzw. der Heilkunde-GmbH an der vertragsärztlichen Versorgung. 2007.

Band 5 Laura Sormani-Bastian: Vergaberecht und Sozialrecht. Unter besonderer Berücksichtigung des Leistungserbringungsrechts im SGB V (Gesetzliche Krankenversicherung). 2007.

Band 6 Marcus Assion: Versicherungsrechtliche Fragen der Lebendspende von Organen. 2007.

Band 7 Yasemin Ilgin: Health Care Expenditures, Innovation, and Demographic Change. 2008.

www.peterlang.de

Peter Lang · Internationaler Verlag der Wissenschaften

Ingrid Zechmeister

Mental Health Care Financing in the Process of Change

Challenges and Approaches for Austria

Frankfurt am Main, Berlin, Bern, Bruxelles, New York, Oxford, Wien, 2005.
183 pp., 19 tab. 13 graf.
Forschungsergebnisse der Wirtschaftsuniversität Wien.
Edited by Wirtschaftsuniversität Wien. Vol. 8
ISBN 978-3-631-54338-2 · pb. € 41.10*

While mental health care has undergone substantial reforms, little attention has been paid to financing issues. This book addresses this shortcoming and brings more transparency into the complex relationship between mental health care reform, service provision and financing. Additionally, it provides rich information about the characteristics of mental health care financing in Western Europe. The author analyses the recent mental health care reform discourse against the backdrop of broader political economic developments and demonstrates the role of financing arrangements herein. The book vividly shows how financing is related to specific effects for service users and their relatives in the process of change. In the final part practitioners, planers and policy makers find useful guidelines for developing alternative financing approaches including support to improve understanding of financing issues amongst those involved in mental health care.

Contents: Perspectives of Mental Illness · Mental Health Care Structures in Austria · Mental Health Care Financing · Paradigm Shift in Mental Health Care: An Exploration of Mental Health Care Reform Objectives and Reform Processes · Mental Health Care Financing in the Light of Reform Objectives and Discourse · Concluding Remarks: What Financing for Mental Health Care?

Frankfurt am Main · Berlin · Bern · Bruxelles · New York · Oxford · Wien
Distribution: Verlag Peter Lang AG
Moosstr. 1, CH-2542 Pieterlen
Telefax 0041 (0) 32/376 17 27

*The €-price includes German tax rate
Prices are subject to change without notice

Homepage http://www.peterlang.de

FSC
www.fsc.org
MIX
Papier | Fördert
gute Waldnutzung
FSC® C083411

Kolibri 360 GmbH
Ferdinand-Jühlke-Straße 7
99095 Erfurt, Deutschland
produktsicherheit@kolibri360.de

Druck:
CPI Druckdienstleistungen GmbH
im Auftrag der
Kolibri 360 GmbH
Ferdinand-Jühlke-Str. 7
99095 Erfurt